LEDLEY KING

LEDLEY KING

THE BIOGRAPHY

IAIN SPRAGG

JOHN BLAKE

Blake Publishing Ltd,
t, 2 Bramber Road,
W14 9PB
England

www.blake.co.uk

First published in hardback in 2008

ISBN 978 1 84454 550 6

British Library Cataloguing-in-Publication Data:

A catalogue record for this book is available from the British Library.

Design by www.envydesign.co.uk

Printed in the UK by CPI William Clowes Ltd, Beccles, NR34 7TL

1 3 5 7 9 10 8 6 4 2

Papers used by John Blake Publishing are natural, recyclable products made from wood grown in sustainable forests. The manufacturing processes conform to the environmental regulations of the country of origin.

Every attempt has been made to contact the relevant copyright-holders, but some were unobtainable. We would be grateful if the appropriate people could contact us.

To Hoolio and the monkeys,
Dylan and Devon

PROLOGUE

When Ledley Brenton King emerged from the famous tunnel at Anfield at half-time in May 1999 to make his Tottenham debut, the unassuming 18-year-old from east London was an unknown teenager with dreams of a professional career and no little nerves.

Eight years later, the boy from Bow is the captain of the club he joined as a 14-year-old, an established England star and widely regarded as one of the best defenders in Europe. This is the story of his remarkable rise to the pinnacle of his profession.

There has always been something refreshingly old-fashioned about King. On the pitch, he is the embodiment of a modern centre-half – athletic, deceptively quick and reassuringly comfortable on the ball. Off the pitch, however, he epitomises a bygone era when footballers were not high-profile multi-millionaires and the pay packet wasn't the highlight of their week. In short, King has never let his considerable success go to his head.

'He's a quiet lad, you hardly notice him, a lovely boy,' said his former Spurs boss David Pleat in 2004. 'He's one of those you wouldn't mind if your daughter married.'

Pleat aside, King has earned himself an army of admirers with his languid yet dynamic performances for club and country and it has been in England colours particularly that he has forged his reputation as a world-class defender.

'I don't like defenders who hold the shirts of other players,' said French striker Thierry Henry in 2006. 'The only defender in England who doesn't do that and sometimes still gets the ball off my feet easily is Ledley King.

'He is the only guy who doesn't hold players. He will get the ball off you without you even noticing. For me, that is a good defender. He plays without contact yet is somehow still strong and gets the ball without doing any fouls.'

Henry should certainly know. The former Arsenal striker came face-to-face with him in the Euro 2004 finals in Portugal. King was drafted into Sven-Göran Eriksson's side at late notice and the way in which the Spurs star nullified the much-vaunted French striker had the critics purring with satisfaction. The Tottenham player simply eclipsed his north London rival from the first to final whistle.

King's story, however, is not one without its share of hardship. He has already experienced more injuries in his career than many players suffer in a lifetime and since his debut against Liverpool, he has played just one full season which has not been blighted by injury.

Each time King has fought his way back without complaint and it speaks volumes about his strength of character that he has returned each time stronger, fitter and even more determined to bring the good times back to White Hart Lane.

By his own admission, the task remains a work in progress. Under his leadership, Spurs have certainly turned the corner and shaken off the malaise that had hung over the club throughout the 1990s. King has been the talisman of this new era for the Lilywhites and as the club's longest-serving player, he is now firmly established as the fans' favourite.

Many believe he is yet to reach his peak and, like a good wine, he has certainly improved with age. His career so far has seen him make the transition from talented teenager to fully-fledged international star with startling ease. What he goes on to achieve in the future for club and country will be a fascinating story in itself.

CONTENTS

1   STREETS OF LONDON   1

2   BAPTISM OF FIRE   11

3   THE MAIN MAN   45

4   THE ITALIAN JOB   83

5   EUROPEAN MISADVENTURE   153

6   KING OF THE LANE   177

7   A NEW HOPE   219

    EPILOGUE   257

    APPENDIX   259

1
STREETS OF LONDON

Although the story of Ledley King's rise to the pinnacle of the professional game, international recognition and the captaincy of his club may not be unique in footballing circles, it is nonetheless one that reveals much about the steely determination that has been the bedrock of the softly-spoken star's career. The odds were certainly not stacked heavily in his favour.

Ledley was born on 12 October 1980 in Bow, in the heart of London's East End. His mother Beverlee worked for the local council and she separated from her partner, Herbert Patterson, before the boy had the chance to know his father. The youngster was not born with a silver spoon in his mouth and he certainly had more than his fair share of challenges to overcome as his mother struggled to raise him and his younger brother Emerson almost single-handedly.

Without a father figure in the home, Beverlee was to prove a huge influence on her eldest son and he has always been quick to pay tribute to the importance of her firm but fair guiding hand in his rise to the top. 'I grew up in a tough area and my mum was quite strict,' he told the *Sunday Times* in 2005. 'She wasn't over the top but she was disciplined about things. She taught me about manners and respect. There were times when I wished I had a little more freedom but, looking back, I'm glad I hadn't. I was allowed to go places but it was on a "once in a blue moon" basis. Luckily enough, I met the right people at the right age and never got drawn into anything wrong.

'My family always encouraged me, put me on the right path and made sure I reached my goals. I don't actually see my dad – it has been my mum, my nan and my grandad who have helped me. You grow up quick in situations like that. I watched my mum struggling to raise me and my brother. As the oldest one, I wanted to help her out as much as possible.'

Fortunately for Beverlee, her young son was already so preoccupied with playing football that it's debatable whether he would have had the time to get into trouble anyway. Ledley lived and breathed the game and the only suggestion of any misbehaviour on his part was the occasional broken ornament in their council flat, the result of his obsessive desire to kick balls. It's unknown whether Beverlee ever found out that he used to glue them back together while she was out at work!

Of course, the confines of the family home were no

place to nurture the talent that was to eventually propel Ledley to the Premiership and he was soon outside developing his skills with other youngsters from the local estate. Beautifully-manicured grass pitches, however, were the stuff of dreams for the young players and they were forced to risk life and limb playing on a concrete pitch just across the way from the flat where he lived. The locals dubbed it 'The Cage' and it was here that Ledley truly began his footballing journey.

'I started in The Cage at a very young age,' he said. 'The games with my mates went on for hours and didn't end until dark. Hamstrings, calf-muscle strains – we never knew about them things.'

It was during these day-long kickabouts that he began to dream about playing the game professionally. Like all children, he already had his football heroes but, surprisingly for a man who was to become such an accomplished central defender, Ledley chose to idolise two players who forged their own reputations further up the pitch.

'I didn't really look at defenders when I was younger,' he admitted in an interview with the *Daily Telegraph*. 'I preferred watching strikers like Marco van Basten and creative players like Paul Gascoigne. Van Basten was the type of player I enjoyed watching. I've always felt it would be nice to be a striker – one of the glory boys.'

By his own admission in those early years, Ledley was never fully convinced he would make it as a professional footballer. He had the talent and the commitment but his natural modesty undermined his confidence. However, there were to be two men in particular who ensured that the youngster would not throw away his chance.

The first was his PE teacher at school, Mr Lyons, who could see the potential in his pupil and was eager to instil the self-belief in him. He knew Ledley suffered from self-doubt and consciously tried to build him up mentally. For a boy who was not setting the world alight academically, it was a vote of confidence that made a lasting impression.

'He had worked in the school for some time and had seen a lot of good players,' Ledley recalled years later. 'He told me he thought I had something special and that can have a big effect on a young person. I tried not to let it go to my head but he gave me quite a lot of confidence. I could have done better at school but football always came first.'

The second figure to play a central role in Ledley's development was Fred Carter. He was the father of James, a close friend of Ledley and a 'Cage' team-mate, and while it was Lyons who tried to bolster Ledley's self-esteem, it was Fred Carter who provided the invaluable practical support. He was the man who did the driving.

At the age of nine, Ledley and James Carter were invited to train with Leyton Orient and it was James's dad who ferried the two young hopefuls to and from the sessions. It was Ledley's first exposure to a professional club and it was a move that would ultimately lead him to Spurs and finally England.

Fred Carter, for one, was in absolutely no doubt that his son's close friend would make it one day. 'Ledley was a natural from the start,' he told the *Daily Mail*. 'I'd pick him up, or he would be staying at our house, and he would forget his boots but when he stepped out on to that football pitch he was a totally different person. He was assured, in control and you did not have to tell him anything. Ledley is now where he was meant to be.'

At the same time as he was spotted by Leyton Orient's scouts, Ledley opted to join a Sunday League side by the name of Senrab FC. He didn't know it at the time, but it was a decision that would have a fundamental impact on his career. Senrab is based at Wanstead Flats in east London. It was founded by the late Bill Payne in 1960 and, during Ledley's time with the club, it ran junior sides for boys from the age of five to seventeen. The pitches are adjacent to the City of London Cemetery and it was here that Ledley was to play alongside a generation of youngsters who would go on to light up the Premiership.

To describe Senrab at that time as a hotbed for young talent would be a gross understatement. The club was positively teeming with future professional stars and, with the benefit of hindsight, Ledley was fortunate to line-up alongside so many gifted players. Chelsea skipper John Terry, Fulham's Paul Konchesky, Bolton's Jlloyd Samuel, West Ham's Bobby Zamora and future White Hart Lane team-mate Jermain Defoe all came through the Senrab ranks and Ledley was determined not to be left behind.

'We were just East End lads coming together and making a good team,' Ledley told the *Daily Telegraph* when he remembered those formative years in the shadow of the nearby graveyard. 'The name Senrab comes from Barnes spelt backwards; I don't know why. I was with the club from the age of nine until fourteen and they were good times. Lee Bowyer played for Senrab before me and Ashley Cole played for our rivals Puma. We had some good games against them.

'The pitches at Wanstead Flats weren't the best but that wasn't important to us. We just wanted to play. I have always been single-minded, always wanted to be a footballer. Growing up in London, there could have been distractions but my friends never got themselves into trouble, which helped me.'

Unsurprisingly, Senrab swept all before them with such an array of talent and, in the 1994/95 season, the Under-15 side claimed every honour on offer in the local Echo League. 'It was my job to get the best side possible,' Senrab coach Paul Rolls told the *Daily Mail*. 'We would go around and see other Sunday teams and, if there were good boys playing for them, we would invite them over. I have never heard of so many boys to come out of one side and progress like they did for this one and I don't think it will happen again. Nowadays, clubs have their Academies and do not let the youngsters play for Sunday league sides.

'When we used to walk out for, say, a Sunday Cup Final, the other team would say, "There is John Terry or Bobby Zamora." The other kids used to look up to them even then. I would tell my players, "You've beaten them already."

'Ledley was an unbelievable centre-half at a young age. He was very laid back. He would never open his mouth and I used to get hold of him and tell him to shout – to make him into a leader. He was a quiet lad but if there was a 50-50 ball to be won, he would leave the other kids standing.'

Although Ledley was still with Leyton Orient, Senrab's

6

reputation was growing and it was not long before the watchful scouts from the bigger clubs were in regular attendance on Sundays to cast their eye over Rolls' young charges. The trips were not wasted. Ledley was now at a crossroads in his career. Orient had invested in him from a young age but it was already obvious he was destined for greater things and the big question was which top-flight side would win the race to secure his services. In the end, it was Tottenham and, in 1995, aged 14, Ledley King signed schoolboy forms with the club. The teenager from the East End was on his way to White Hart Lane and stardom.

The next major influence on the youngster was to be Spurs youth team coach Pat Holland, the former West Ham United midfielder, who was to oversee Ledley's development from aspiring hopeful to first-team regular. Initially, Ledley's innate shyness made it difficult for him to adapt to life at Spurs. Surrounded by new team-mates and occasionally training with the star names in the first-team squad, he felt out of his depth, but Holland doggedly focused on bolstering the teenager's confidence. Slowly but surely, Ledley's star quality and footballing prowess began to emerge.

It was during this period that he spent five weeks on holiday with relatives in Jamaica. It was an experience that had a lasting effect on the young man and he admitted it helped him to stop worrying about his new life at the Lane. 'It was a culture shock,' he said. 'To go to the toilet, you had to go outside the house. It made me appreciate what I had in Stepney, where I grew up.'

The move to Tottenham also thrust him into the

reckoning for an international call-up and, in September 1996, he was selected to played for the England Under-16s in a friendly game against France. The match ended in a 1–0 defeat for the English youngsters but Ledley was beginning to forge a growing reputation for himself for both club and country.

He won his second Under-16 cap the following month in a 2–2 draw against a talented Czech Republic side in a European Championship qualifier. Two days later, he was picked again for another qualifier against Spain and, although England were comprehensively outplayed by the Spanish in a 5–1 defeat, Ledley was one of the few in the side to shine.

He was to play for the Under-16s once more – a goalless draw against Sweden in February 1997 – but it was back at White Hart Lane, under Holland's patient tutelage, that he was now beginning to show signs that he would become a real star. The club were acutely aware of his potential and it came as little surprise when he traded in his schoolboy forms for a trainee contract in July that year. Tottenham were clearly determined not to let their rough diamond leave.

Spurs were developing an exciting crop of youngsters at the time and Ledley was at the forefront. 'Ledley's not quite the new Sol Campbell,' said Holland in 1998, 'but he's an exceptional prospect.' Holland's young side battled through to the play-off final of the FA Premier Youth League that season and, once again, Ledley was outstanding.

The summer of 1998 was to be another watershed in Ledley's life. With his 18th birthday looming, it was time for Spurs to decide whether to offer him his first professional contract. With the benefit of hindsight, the club would have been insane not to sign him but the teenager still had to endure sleepless nights before Tottenham asked him to put pen to paper. Ledley was to join the senior ranks and, although he probably thought he would have to bide his time before breaking into the first team, his début was to come sooner than he could have imagined.

Before his senior début for the club, however, there was further international recognition for the youngster when he was selected for the England Under-18 squad to play in the European Championship finals in Spain in February 1999.

The squad featured future full internationals Joe Cole, Scott Parker, Darius Vassell and Wayne Bridge and, in the three matches in which Ledley featured – against Spain, Andorra and Israel – England were unbeaten, scoring 11 goals and conceding just twice. His Under-18s exploits were another important phase in his football education but his real rite of passage would come in the Spurs first team.

Three short months later, Ledley was to face his baptism of fire.

2

BAPTISM
OF FIRE

The 1998/99 season was far from a vintage one in the history of Tottenham. Swiss manager Christian Gross had been sacked after just three Premiership games, less than a year after he had succeeded Gerry Francis and, although the appointment of ex-Arsenal manager George Graham had temporarily galvanised the team, Spurs were languishing in mid-table anonymity as the season drew to an underwhelming anticlimax.

Victory in the Worthington Cup Final over Leicester at Wembley in March had given the White Hart Lane faithful something to cheer about, albeit briefly, but the sense that the team had failed to deliver in the Premiership hung over the side.

For Ledley, the campaign had been one of consolidation in the reserve team. He was now 18 years old but, despite his massive potential and impressive performances for the England Under-18s, there seemed to be no rush to blood him in the first team. He was the future and Graham appeared content to allow him to continue to learn his trade away from the spotlight.

Then in March 1999, Graham's hand was forced. Spurs faced a season-defining FA Cup semi-final clash with Newcastle at Old Trafford. The manager had been hit with a spate of injuries, including Swiss defender Ramon Vega and, as the big game approached, he cast his experienced eye over the reserves for cover. King was the obvious choice and Graham had no hesitation in naming the teenager on the bench for Tottenham's biggest game of the season.

The match was a thriller that went into nerve-jangling extra-time but it was ultimately Newcastle who reached the Final after two goals from Alan Shearer. The disappointment for Graham and Spurs was palpable but, for Ledley, it was another huge personal step forward. He had made the all-important 16 for the first time in his career and, although he had to endure Spurs' exit helplessly from the bench, it was a step up from anything he had experienced with the reserves. He was now on the verge of the big breakthrough.

It did not, however, come in the team's next game, a league trip to the City Ground to face Nottingham Forest. Graham's injury problems had eased and Ledley dropped out of contention.

In fact, he had to wait until the following month to make the bench once again. It was another north-western destination but this time it was for the Premiership clash with Liverpool. If he was to make his Tottenham début, it would not come at a more intimidating place than Anfield. Spurs had not beaten the Reds on Merseyside for six years and expectations of ending the losing sequence were far from sky high.

The match, on 1 May 1999, could not, however, have started better for the visitors. An own-goal after 13 minutes from Jamie Carragher put Spurs in front and, when Steffen Iversen added a second ten minutes before the break, an unlikely upset seemed a genuine possibility.

And then their luck changed. Graham's side seemed on the verge of heading into the dressing room for half-time with a two-goal lead when Argentinian full-back Mauricio Taricco was shown a second yellow card for an innocuous-looking challenge on Steve McManaman. Tottenham now faced the prospect of a full 45 minutes with ten men and 44,000 Liverpool fans screaming for goals.

At half-time, Graham was forced to consider his options. With winger David Ginola, midfielders Ruel Fox and Tim Sherwood and second-choice keeper Espen Baardsen as four of his five substitutes, Ledley was the obvious choice to strengthen the defence in readiness for the anticipated Liverpool onslaught. Midfielder Stephen Clemence was sacrificed to make way for him and the 18-year-old proudly ran out for the second-half at Anfield. He was now a fully-fledged professional, playing Premiership football.

Some great players have great débuts but it's safe to say Ledley will not remember his first 45 minutes for Tottenham fondly. Not that he was personally embarrassed, but Liverpool were clearly stung by what had happened in the first half and came out with real conviction.

Future Spurs captain Jamie Redknapp scored Liverpool's first from the penalty spot; Paul Ince claimed the equaliser and McManaman delivered the coup de grâce 11 minutes from the end. Tottenham's ten men had been unable to hold the home team at bay and Ledley's début ended in defeat.

'My début should have been the fulfilment of a dream but it turned into a nightmare for the team,' he told the *Sunday Mirror* two years later. 'We lost 3–2 and I was wondering whether that would be it for me at the back.'

The last of three games of the season saw Spurs beaten by Arsenal and Manchester United without Ledley being involved but he was back on the bench for a 2–2 draw with Chelsea at White Hart Lane. Modest progress, admittedly, but the teenager was beginning to make his mark on the senior set-up.

The summer of 1999 did not bring good news. Although Ledley had taken his first tentative steps to establishing himself as first-team player, Graham was busy in the transfer market and his new back four recruits seemed to suggest that the youngster would have to bide his time in the reserves. In all, Graham bought three central defenders: Chris Perry was lured away from Wimbledon in a £4 million deal; Gary Doherty was signed from Luton for £1 million; and youngster Anthony Gardner was prised away from Port Vale in another £1 million deal. Graham still also had the experience of Sol

Campbell, John Scales and Vega to call on in the heart of his defence, so Ledley had effectively dropped down the Tottenham pecking order without even kicking a ball.

The start of the 1999/00 season only served to confirm his fears. Three consecutive Premiership wins cheered the fans but Ledley watched the games from the stands after failing to make the bench, and he would have been forgiven for wondering when his next serious outing would be.

As it transpired, it would be in the white of England rather than Spurs. Howard Wilkinson was the England Under-21 manager and he decided to call Ledley into his side to face Luxembourg at Reading for a European Championship qualifier in September. Still just 18 years old, he was back in the England fold.

The game itself was predictably one-sided against one of the minnows of European football and England rattled in five goals courtesy of Steven Gerrard, Francis Jeffers, Lee Hendrie, Carl Cort and Frank Lampard. More significantly, England kept a clean sheet and Ledley returned to White Hart Lane safe in the knowledge he had given George Graham a timely reminder of his talents.

Perhaps the manager had sent someone from the club to watch him because, the following month, Ledley was back in the first team just four days after celebrating his 19th birthday. The match was a Premiership clash with Derby County at Pride Park and this time Graham decided to include the teenager from the start. He was to make his full début for the club, although he was deployed in the Spurs midfield rather than the middle of the back four. It was to set the pattern of his early White Hart Lane career, with Graham frequently opting to play him in front of the defence.

'George always saw me as a holding midfield player,' Ledley admitted after the Scotsman's departure from White Hart Lane in March 2001. 'I wanted to play in a more central defensive role. Frankly, he thought my heading was poor and thought it would be a problem in this position. But I can't be too hard on George because he gave me my big break.'

For Graham's part, he was adamant that Ledley's long-term future lay somewhere not too far from the centre circle. 'Tall midfielders are a great asset,' the Spurs boss said. 'Ledley is in the same mould as Patrick Vieira and Marcel Desailly, who was such an outstanding midfielder when he played for Milan before joining Chelsea and establishing himself at centre-half. What I like about Ledley is that he's so composed on the ball – wins it, passes it and gets around the field really well for such a big lad. He can play centre-half as well, and that was his original position. But I've looked at his strengths and weaknesses and I know that midfield is his best position.'

If Ledley's first taste of first-team football at Anfield the previous season had been a rude awakening to the reality of life in the Premiership, the next match at Pride Park was an altogether different experience which, if not exactly a fairytale, was certainly a more confidence-building experience. In the end, the game was settled by a single goal – Chris Armstrong's diving header in the first half enough to seal the three points – and Ledley looked assured as the holding man in midfield, providing the platform for the likes of Ginola to take the game to the Rams. Although he may still have secretly been yearning for his chance in the heart of the defence, he had shown his manager, his team-mates and the Spurs fans that he was more than capable of doing a job for the side.

Sadly, fate then conspired to rob him of the chance to build on his performance against Derby. Initially, a niggling but far from serious knee injury kept him out of the first-team reckoning and, when that had cleared up, he broke a bone in his foot on his comeback in a reserve team game. The teenager was to be sidelined for six long months with the injury and, although he was to make a full recovery, it was still a significant setback in his fledgling career.

There was little choice but to knuckle down, wait for the bone to heal and then start working on his fitness. Periods of enforced inactivity are frustrating even for seasoned professionals who accept injury as an occupational hazard but, for Ledley, the months were tortuous. He had two first-team appearances to his name and now his chance of staking a claim for a regular place had been snatched from him.

It was not until the end of 1999/00 season that he was finally ready to play again and he was to feature in the club's final two games of the campaign. Tottenham's penultimate match was against Manchester United at Old Trafford – the scene of his squad début on the Spurs bench almost a year earlier – and, after such a long lay-off, Graham decided to name him as a substitute with a view to giving him some much-needed time on the pitch during the second-half.

United had already wrapped up the Premiership title but any hopes Spurs had of the home side exuding a little end-of-season charity were dashed in a first half that saw the champions score three while Tottenham replied with a Chris Armstrong goal. There were to be no more goals after the break and, in the end, Ledley had to wait until the 84th minute before shedding his tracksuit and replacing Matthew Etherington. It was an unimportant six minutes of action in terms of the game but, for the player, it represented the end of what had been an incredibly difficult six months. Injury free at last, Ledley King was back.

The final game of the season saw Sunderland visit White Hart Lane and Graham, mindful of the amount of football his young player had missed, was clearly eager to get the teenager back into the thick of the action. Ledley was named in the starting XI at left-back in a back four of Stephen Carr, Sol Campbell and Chris Perry and, despite his lack of match fitness, he lasted the full 90 minutes. Spurs won the game 3–1 and, albeit in a modest way, he had finished the season on a high. He was still very much a novice in terms of top-flight experience, but he was edging closer and closer to a regular place.

There was however even better news just around the corner. Despite just three appearances in the first team that season and his frustrating injury problems, Howard Wilkinson made the decision to include him in his Under-21 squad for the European Championship finals in

Slovakia. Ledley's burgeoning reputation went before him and Wilkinson was obviously determined to have the powerful teenager involved.

'It was a shock, but a pleasant one, to be called into the squad,' Ledley admitted as he prepared to board the plane for Slovakia. 'I haven't played much at all this season and I'm grateful to be in contention. When I was out injured, Howard showed me he was interested in me and kept up to date with me. He's known me from the Under-18s as well, so he's watched my progress for some time. I'm really looking forward to the competition and hopefully I can do well out there. If I get a chance, I'll be looking to impress.'

He was joined in the Under-21 squad by fellow Spurs youngster Luke Young and the group flew out with high hopes. England's tournament began against the highly-rated Italians in the Slovakian capital Bratislava. It would prove to be a stern test of the credentials of Wilkinson's side and despite Ledley's modest assertion that he would have to settle for a place on the England bench, he was named in the starting line-up.

Sadly, the match did not go according to plan and, despite some periods of dominance, England's young lions were beaten 2–0. The tournament had begun in the worst possible fashion. There was little time, however, for the players to dwell on the result as they were to play Turkey in their second group game just two days later. It was now make or break time and, after a quick post mortem of his team's performance against the Italians, Wilkinson settled on his side to face Turkey. He resisted the temptation to make sweeping changes and Ledley was once again paired with Liverpool's Jamie Carragher in the middle of the defence.

Fortunately for England, Turkey were not in the same class as Italy and the team quickly shrugged off the disappointment of defeat to produce a polished and mature display. England scored a total of six unanswered goals from Frank Lampard, Francis Jeffers, Carl Cort, Danny Mills, Andy Campbell and a certain Ledley Brenton King, converting David Dunn's cross in the 72nd minute. It was his first ever goal in England colours and had come in only his third appearance for the Under-21s.

Victory gave the team renewed hope of progressing to the next stage of the tournament and it was little surprise when Wilkinson decided to stick with the King–Carragher partnership for the all-important final group game against hosts Slovakia. The pair were now the obvious first-choice centre-back combination and the manager was relying on them to give his side the platform from which they could go on and win the match.

It was not to be. Once again, England acquitted themselves well but a technically adept Slovakian side seemed to relish playing in front of their own fans in Bratislava and scored twice through Peter Babnic and Szilard Nemeth in a devastating seven-minute spell that settled the outcome. England were consigned to third place in the group and an early flight home.

'We played against a good side in very difficult conditions – a full stadium, very enthusiastic fans – a metaphorical lion's den,' Wilkinson said after the match. 'The achievements of the players who got us to this tournament and those we've brought here must not be underestimated. The 12 players who can play next year from this squad and the two who can play the year after will, I hope, have learned an enormous amount from this tournament.' He went on to say that the results had been disappointing, but that winning games at Under-21 level wasn't everything. The bigger picture also had to be acknowledged – the development of a new crop of England stars, who would be ready to grace the international arena at the highest level, and at the top of their game.

For Ledley, the 'bigger picture' was depressingly mixed. Although he had been a lynchpin of the side and enhanced his reputation despite England's premature elimination, he once again broke his foot, this time in the final minute of the Slovakia game, and just as it had seemed he was destined for an injury-free pre-season and a concerted assault on the first team, he was suddenly facing another period of rehabilitation. The news would have devastated lesser men, but the 19-year-old accepted his fate and reported back to White Hart Lane to begin his recovery.

At least the club did not add insult to injury over the summer by buying another raft of defensive rein-forcements as they had the previous year. In fact, George Graham limited his purchases to recruiting Ben Thatcher from Wimbledon and, with centre-half John Scales allowed to sign for Ipswich on a free, it appeared the defensive status quo at White Hart Lane had not fundamentally changed.

Of course, Ledley still faced a battle on two fronts. First, he had to get himself fit and physically ready for first-team football. But he also had to try to convince his manager that his best position was in his favoured central defence rather than midfield. The battle of wills was one played out discreetly on the club training ground rather than in the full glare of the newspapers but, ultimately, it would take a dramatic turn of events for Ledley finally to get his wish.

Before he could concentrate on staking his claim at White Hart Lane, he was back in England colours for the Under-21s. Five months of hard work on the training ground were finally behind him and Wilkinson named Ledley in his side to face Italy, the reigning European champions, in Monza at the beginning of November. It was to be his first appearance for club or country since the heartbreak of defeat to Slovakia.

The game itself was not what anyone could have anticipated as the weather conspired to make a mockery of the fixture. Heavy fog made visibility a real problem at kick-off and, just minutes after the start, the Bulgarian referee pulled both sides off and waited to see if the conditions would improve. They briefly made it back out but, after 11 minutes, it was time to call a halt to proceedings and abandon the game. Ledley's comeback had lasted barely more than ten minutes.

'It is very disappointing but, in the circumstances, I don't know what else the referee could do,' Wilkinson said after the bizarre end to the match. 'The fog just seemed to come down quickly and completely carpet the pitch. I thought the referee was right in coming off for five minutes and I said to him we will go along with any decision you make.' Wilkinson also pointed out the risk of injury from warming up and warming down, as well as the simple fact of players not being able to see each other. The manager added, 'Apparently, Ledley King and one of their players went for a ball and the referee completely lost sight of it.'

Five days after the débâcle in Italy, however, Ledley was ready to play club football again. His rehabilitation had gone according to plan but the same could not be said for the club during his absence. A third-round Worthington Cup defeat to Birmingham in October had already fanned the flames of discontent among the Tottenham faithful and, by the time the team were due to entertain Liverpool at White Hart Lane – Ledley's comeback game – there were disgruntled supporters distributing leaflets outside the ground urging chairman Sir Alan Sugar to sell his shares because of his perceived lack of investment. George Graham's honeymoon period as manager was well and truly over and the atmosphere was tense.

Ledley was again deployed in midfield but there was little he could do to prevent Robbie Fowler opening the scoring for the visitors after just 18 minutes. Things looked bleak for Spurs and Ledley was enduring a testing return to first-team action. But roared on by the 30,000 Spurs fans who had temporarily forgotten their grievances, the side steeled themselves and, when Les Ferdinand scored from close range, they were back on terms and back in the match. Tim Sherwood added a second with a crashing header four minutes before the break and, although it was a nervous second half, they clung on for the three points that Graham, the team and the club desperately needed. The ongoing crisis was not over but it had certainly been averted for the time being.

It spoke volumes about Ledley's natural athleticism and stamina that he was able to last the full 90 minutes against Liverpool after his five-month lay-off. The pace of the game was frenetic but he lasted the distance and he was now ready for his first extended run in the first team. He still had a mere five league appearances to his name yet the team already felt below strength without his muscular presence.

A convincing victory over Leicester City and a defeat at Old Trafford against Manchester United followed, before the Spurs were to face Bradford at Valley Parade in December. Ledley was named in the side again but little could he have imagined he would be making Premiership history almost as soon as the referee Neale Barry blew his whistle.

Just seconds after kick-off, he received the ball in the Bradford half and strode towards goal. The defence backed off and Ledley decided to try his luck and unleashed a powerful 25-yard effort that was hit with real venom. His luck was certainly in because the shot deflected off Bantams defender Robert Molenaar and sailed past 'keeper Matthew Clarke into the back of the net. The goal was timed at 11 seconds, which remains a Premiership record for the quickest goal ever scored in a league fixture. The previous best was 13 seconds, set jointly by Blackburn's Chris Sutton in 1994 and Aston Villa's Dwight Yorke the following year. Ledley had scored his first goal for his club in the most spectacular fashion and, although he would credit his achievement to a 'wicked deflection', it later nevertheless made people sit up and take notice of the youngster.

There was, however, little time for him to rest on his laurels and, if the match had started in explosive style for Tottenham, it was to end in disappointment and recrimination.

Bradford drew level just eight minutes later, but Spurs established a 3–1 lead courtesy of Sol Campbell and Chris Armstrong, and seemed to be on course for three much-needed points away from home. The home side had other ideas, though, with Dean Windass reducing the deficit on 69 minutes to set up a grandstand finish. Spurs' nerves were palpable as the clock ticked down; the Bantams laid siege to Neil Sullivan's goal and, in the 89th minute, they found a way through as Italian striker Benito Carbone hooked home a dramatic equaliser. Spurs had snatched a meagre draw from the jaws of victory.

'Although it was great to score my first senior goal, the record doesn't mean that much to me to be honest,' Ledley admitted after the game. 'It is a lovely bonus. But the most important thing for me is to get more matches in the side and try and establish myself.'

For Graham, the final result was something approaching a disaster. 'It was clearly two points lost,' he observed bitterly after the final whistle. 'We appeared comfortable when our third goal went in, but we couldn't handle things when Bradford adopted a more direct approach in the last 20 minutes or so. I cannot fault the players for their effort. If we are eventually going down, we will go down fighting. However, if it's spirit and determination that is required to stay up, we have it.'

Talk of relegation so early in the campaign was certainly not what the fans wanted to hear and a vocal minority of supporters made their feelings about the manager clear. Tottenham were on the ropes and with Arsenal, Graham's former club, the visitors to White Hart Lane for the north London derby the following week, there seemed little respite on the horizon. It was time for the players to stand up and be counted.

It was to be Ledley's first experience of the white-hot atmosphere of the derby and, although he had only turned 20 a few short weeks before the big game, he exuded a calm confidence when asked about what he expected of the occasion. 'I've grown up watching these local derbies and played in a few at youth and reserve level,' he said. 'Even those are a bit special. I'm really looking forward to the match and hopefully we can get the right result.'

The derby was seven days before Christmas but there was precious little seasonal goodwill on display at White Hart Lane as the two old rivals tore into each other with the obligatory gusto. Two players had seen red and a further nine had been shown the yellow card in the fixture the previous season and it was no surprise that the first foul of the match was committed with just 15 seconds on the clock.

Genuine threats on goal were scarce in the opening first half-hour until Darren Anderton unleashed a stinging shot from long range which the Arsenal 'keeper Alex Manninger could only parry. Ukrainian striker Sergei Rebrov was perfectly placed to capitalise on the rebound and Spurs found themselves one up.

As the game progressed into the second-half, Ledley found himself under siege in midfield as Arsenal pressed desperately for the equaliser, and his heroics seemed to be paying off as the match headed for the final minute. But it was not to be and, when Patrick Vieira rose unchallenged to meet a late corner, Neil Sullivan was beaten and Tottenham were once again left to rue being pegged back in the dying minutes for the second successive match. The two rivals shared the spoils but, for Tottenham, it felt like a defeat.

The hangover from the Arsenal clash obviously affected the team and the remainder of the festive period was not a happy one. A draw at White Hart Lane against Middlesbrough was nothing to celebrate and successive defeats on the road to Southampton and Ipswich only served to increase the pressure on the beleaguered manager and his players.

The Tottenham cause was not helped by the growing media speculation that club chairman Sir Alan Sugar was poised to sell his shares and walk away from the Lane. The story refused to go away and the player found themselves constantly questioned by the press about the situation.

With things going badly awry on the pitch, it was the

last thing the squad, particularly the younger players like Ledley, needed and it fell on the gnarled professionals like Les Ferdinand to try and deflect the media attention away from his junior team-mates. 'If you start worrying about what's happening off the field, you tend to lose the plot on the pitch. We'll just leave it up to the suits,' Ferdinand said. 'The team is taking shape but George says he still needs two, three or four more players. The current players are going to give all that they've got, while Ledley King and Alton Thelwell have been two real finds and a few more youngsters will come through and make the grade.' He also pointed out that the fans desperately wanted to see their home-grown players, particularly, given opportunities to shine. He warned, though, that retaining players like Darren Anderton and Sol Campbell was critical to the club making any kind of progress.

While the off-field politics raged, Spurs prepared for the arrival of Newcastle at White Hart Lane on 2 January. Tottenham's last victory in the league had been against Leicester in November and a victory was of paramount importance. To describe the game as dramatic would be a massive understatement. The Spurs faithful were at their vocal best; the atmosphere was akin to a Cup tie and the events that unfolded were as entertaining as they were controversial.

Newcastle took the lead through Nolberto Solano midway through the second half but five more goals, three penalties and three sending-offs followed and, at the end of 90 adrenalin-fuelled minutes of play, Spurs emerged 4–2 victors.

Ledley, however, found himself at the centre of the post-match debate after the referee refused to award Newcastle a penalty after his debatable challenge on Christian Bassedas in the area. He escaped without censure but the incident was replayed in minute detail after the game and Magpies boss Sir Bobby Robson was uncharacteristically critical of the decision in his port-match interview. For Ledley, the three points were all that mattered and Spurs had earned themselves a little breathing space.

The next game was a third-round FA Cup trip to Leyton Orient – the first professional club to show an interest in Ledley and the one he had to leave at the age of 14 to further his career. It would be an emotional return to Brisbane Road, but with Tottenham still mired in boardroom manoeuvrings, a poor run of form and a mounting injury crisis, he knew there would be no room for sentiment. Spurs were still striving for the first away win of the campaign and failure to dispose of the lower league opposition could have serious consequences.

In truth, Tottenham were far from convincing against Orient. The first half was a turgid affair only briefly brought to life when King rose to meet an Oyvind Leonhardsen cross with a powerful header, only to see his effort smash against the crossbar and bounce to safety. The second 45 minutes were little better and, ultimately, Spurs were extremely lucky to come away with the spoils after Gary Doherty scored in injury-time. A win was a win but the performance did little to allay the fears of those who believed the team could yet be sucked into an unseemly relegation battle.

Those concerns significantly grew over the next month. Four successive goalless draws in the Premiership saw the side slip further into trouble and the lack of goals – or the flowing football that was part of the long tradition of the club – only heightened the sense of anxiety and disenchantment among the supporters.

The only cause for optimism seemed to be the assured performances of the Tottenham youngsters like Ledley. 'If you look at the likes of King, Doherty and Thelwell and people like [Simon] Davies and [Matthew] Etherington – they've all had an involvement,' said reserve team coach Chris Hughton. 'This is the most amount of players we've had that are on the fringes of the first team. That has been down the injuries we've had and the fact that we haven't the biggest squad but, for whatever reason, it has been a wonderful benefit for those lads.' Hughton went on to acknowledge that there was a great deal of pressure being applied to some of those young players, who felt they had to prove themselves instantly if they were to stand a chance of remaining in or around the first-team squad. But the pressure was not necessarily negative in every case. 'I'm absolutely delighted with how the lads have done. Sometimes they are in by default, sometimes injury, sometimes by their own endeavours.

The most important thing is that reserve team players here can see light at the end of the tunnel.'

After their toothless performances in the league, the team had the welcome-distraction of an FA Cup fourth-round clash at Charlton at the start of February and George Graham decided to make a significant tactical change to his line-up, naming Ledley in a back three alongside Sol Campbell and Chris Perry. His patience had finally been rewarded and he would start the match where he felt most at home.

The early exchanges at the Valley saw Tottenham's defensive trio pierced twice as Charlton went two goals up, but Spurs finally found their shooting boots and goals from Darren Anderton, Leonhardsen and Rebrov, as well Richard Rufus' own goal, ensured a handsome 4–2 victory and a place in the next round.

'It's been going well for me in midfield but I thought I did all right at Charlton at the back,' Ledley told the club's official website after the game. 'As long as I'm playing that's the main thing. I suppose you could call that a typical Cup tie. Charlton started well but I thought we were brilliant in the end after being 2–0 down. To be fair, I didn't think we ever believed we were out of it. We were still creating chances and we knew that if we could pull one goal back we could go out and get another and that's exactly what happened.

'They only had one chance in the first half and scored from it and we just had to keep doing what we were doing. Obviously, it was then difficult when they scored again but we stuck at it and got what we deserved.'

Spurs were drawn at home to Stockport County in the fifth round later the same month and, this time, there was to be no repeat of the stuttering performance against lower league opposition that had set the alarm bells ringing at Leyton Orient.

The team was at its potent best at White Hart Lane and

it was Ledley who got the ball rolling in the fifth minute of the match with his second goal for the club. It wasn't quite as quick as his effort at Bradford two months earlier, but it settled any nerves there were and the side strolled to a 4–0 win. The Cup run was now gathering real momentum and Ledley was able to report for England Under-21 duty safe in the knowledge that his club finally appeared to be turning the corner.

The Under-21 game was at Birmingham's St Andrews ground against Spain and, although it was only a friendly, the match had an extra significance for Ledley, who was keenly aware of the last time he had crossed swords with the Spanish.

'I've played Spain once before at Under-16 level and they managed to beat us 5–1. I haven't forgotten that and I'm sure some of the lads who will be there this time won't have forgotten either,' he said in the build-up to the game. 'Playing for England is the best feeling ever. When you put on the shirt and you are singing the national anthem, it is the best feeling.' Ledley added that he knew he had only got his chance with the national team because Gareth Barry pulled out, but was philosophical about grabbing his opportunity. 'I enjoyed it thoroughly. I managed to score a goal and the tournament was very enjoyable and a good learning process.' The nagging doubts about injuries, even at this stage in his career, were never completely banished, but he recognised that as long as he remained injury-free, there was no reason why he should not be a long-term fixture in the side.

Ledley had to settle for a place on the bench against

Spain but any thoughts he had of gaining revenge for his Under-16 pain were quickly dispelled as the visitors hit four past England and, although he was brought on in the second-half, it was another Spanish encounter he would want to forget.

Returning to White Hart Lane the following day, Ledley probably hoped for a quiet moment to reflect on the disappointment in Birmingham but fate conspired against him when the news filtered out that Sir Alan Sugar had resigned as chairman after selling shares worth more than £209 million to sports and media group Enic. The club was in the full glare of the media spotlight once again and there seemed to be no hiding place.

The players were naturally hounded by a media desperate for insider gossip and speculation, but they tried as far as possible to keep their heads down. It was an uncertain time as the new owners took control of the club and, despite the public protestations from all concerned that it was business as usual, there was a distinct air of uncertainty.

Fortunately for King, the new regime seemed intent on proving to the supporters exactly what their intentions were and, just two days before the crucial quarter-final clash with West Ham at Upton Park, it was announced that the club was extending his contract. The message was crystal clear – the new owners valued homegrown players and Ledley King was a fundamental part of their future plans.

'Ledley has made good progress this season,' said director of football David Pleat. 'His opportunities have come from injuries, but he has proved he can handle the senior team, which is a massive bonus to the manager. It is very unfair to treat him as a very junior professional and he was getting very junior professional salaries. His contract wasn't expiring at the end of the season and that is the act of good faith we have showed to him.'

The youngster could not have received a more glowing endorsement in the build-up to the West Ham game and it was obvious the resounding vote of confidence bolstered his confidence and allowed him to relish the showdown with some familiar faces in the Hammers line-up. 'I've grown up playing against the likes of Joe [Cole] and Michael [Carrick] and have played in the England Under-21s with Frank [Lampard]. In fact, I had a little chat with Frank the day before the quarter-final draw and we said that we would play each other,' he said. 'He said they wouldn't have a problem with us but I told him otherwise.' Ledley, of course, also had his eyes on the path that had been trodden by those particular players – the one that led directly into the heart of the England set-up. He knew it could be done by players who had come up through the ranks, and was determined that he would follow in their footsteps – sooner rather than later. For the moment, though, he was willing to bide his time, and take his opportunities when they presented themselves. Privately, he set himself the goal of achieving England call-up status within a couple of seasons.

With his international aspirations fuelled by his new contract and Spurs' solid Cup run, Ledley could not have been in a better frame of mind for what was the biggest club game of his fledgling career. The game itself was everything a Cup tie, not to mention a London derby, should be. He was back in the midfield holding role and, although it was Sergei Rebrov who ultimately took the lion's share of the plaudits, courtesy of his two goals in a 3–2 victory, Ledley's assured performance in what was a frenetic battle in the middle of the pitch was outstanding.

The draw for the eagerly anticipated semi-finals saw Spurs paired with Arsenal. The great north London derby was destined for only its fifth ever FA Cup game and the sense of anticipation was electric. 'It's another London derby and an FA Cup semi-final and I couldn't ask for more in my first season,' King told the club website. 'I'm just looking forward to it. The FA Cup games have been amazing. It's my first season in the competition and I've thoroughly enjoyed it.'

Spurs faced a league clash with Coventry before the semi-final, but before King and the rest of the players could start to think ahead to their Arsenal showdown, the club was rocked by the news that George Graham had been sacked. Just five days after their heroics against West Ham, the team were suddenly without their manager.

Graham's departure was a shock. The season's league campaign had been fought in the wrong half of the table and there remained the innate suspicion of a former Arsenal player and manager among the fans, but there was also a feeling that the team, with youngsters like Ledley to the fore, was finally heading in the right direction. The march to the semi-finals of the FA Cup had only strengthened the belief that the Scotsman would be given more time by the club's new owners.

Officially, Graham had been sacked because of a breach of contract, but whatever the real reason behind his abrupt and acrimonious departure, it left the first-team players in limbo. The rumour mill went into overdrive and the appointment of David Pleat as caretaker manager did nothing to dampen down the speculation.

For Ledley, Graham's departure elicited mixed emotions. His reluctance to see him as a natural centre-back was a cause of frustration to the youngster but he was quick to remind the opinion-hungry press that he was also the man who had handed him his début at Anfield less than two years ago. Perhaps more significantly, he was the only manager Ledley had played for during his short professional career and, while the older Spurs players were well versed in the reality of the managerial merry-go-round, it was a new experience for him. Whoever ultimately replaced Graham would be unknown to the 20-year-old and he had no idea whether the new man would have the same faith in his talents as the Scot had shown.

Football, however, waits for no man and just a day after Graham's sacking had been announced, Spurs entertained Coventry at White Hart Lane. The assembled 35,000-strong crowd were clearly anxious to see how the side would respond to the previous day's events but, in the end, they need not have worried.

It is one of football's favourite and arguably most accurate truisms that a team suddenly separated from its manager will react with an inspired, passionate display in their very next game and Tottenham were not about to let the side down as they stormed to a 3–0 victory. The old adage had been proved true once again.

Deployed in midfield, Ledley was in commanding form and he was duly voted the Man of the Match. Anyone who believed the youngster's performance might suffer without Graham's guiding hand was proved wrong. He was, in fact, visibly maturing with every performance and, rather than reflect on the past, he was eager to focus on the future when interviewed about the recent upheaval at the club. 'We want a new manager brought in as soon as possible because it is better for the club,' he told the London *Evening Standard* in the wake of Graham's sacking. 'It has been a bit of a roller-coaster ride at Spurs recently. We were on a high after beating West Ham in the FA Cup and the news of the boss going was disappointing. Graham was a big influence on me and was the manager from when I started to get into the first team. It was sad to see him go.

'It is strange without a manager but we know that happens in football and we just have to get on with it. We all know David Pleat, Stewart Houston is still there, so we still know the people who are around us and what is expected from us.'

Following their morale-boosting victory over Coventry, Spurs faced an enforced two-week lay-off for international games and Ledley was once again called up by the Under-21s for the European Championship qualifier against Finland at Barnsley's Oakwell ground. It was to be his seventh cap for the side and, by now, he was very much an integral figure in the Under-21 set-up.

England cruised to a comfortable victory against the Finns in Barnsley, courtesy of strikes from Darius Vassell, Ledley's old Senrab friend John Terry and a brace from Newcastle youngster Shola Ameobi, but the evening was soured for Ledley when he was forced off with a dead leg. It was not a serious injury but, with crucial club games looming, it was definitely not what the doctor ordered.

As fate would have it, Tottenham were scheduled to face Arsenal at Highbury in the Premiership just a week before their FA Cup showdown. Characteristically, Ledley was chomping at the bit to feature in the second derby match of his career but caretaker boss Pleat decided at the 11th hour that it was not worth the risk and Ledley was left out of the squad. His disappointment was understandable but Pleat's decision only underlined Ledley's growing stature in the team. He was increasing perceived as a 'big-match' player whom Tottenham simply had to have fighting fit for the big Cup clash.

There's no doubt Ledley's combative presence and coolness in possession were sorely missed in the Highbury dress rehearsal and, although an under-strength side stemmed the Arsenal tide for much of the match, two goals in the last 20 minutes from the home side broke their resistance and Tottenham were beaten.

Normally, a derby defeat would cast a shadow over White Hart Lane for days, but the players, the club and fans had little time to wallow in their collective misery. Tottenham were about to unveil their new manager.

The announcement of a big club's coach invariably generates excitement and a sense of renewed optimism.

The news that Glenn Hoddle was returning to White Hart Lane fourteen years after his last game for the club as a player sent the fans into a frenzy. One of Spurs' favourite sons was coming home.

As a player, Hoddle seemed to be the living embodiment of everything that Tottenham stood for. Stylish, elegant and outrageously talented, he played over 400 times for the club and he was the creative hub of the side that won the FA Cup in 1981 and 1982 and the team that claimed the 1984 UEFA Cup. The White Hart Lane faithful could not have had any fonder memories of Hoddle and welcomed him back as the new manager with open arms and high expectations. They certainly didn't care that Southampton were far from pleased at him leaving them to take the job.

'It's emotional and exciting to return,' Hoddle admitted in the press conference that followed his appointment. 'I've spent many years here and the supporters have given me a superb reception. I first walked through the gates of this club at age eight as a supporter and left when I was 29. That's a huge part of my life.

'Spurs have always had a style. In an ideal world, that is what we want but you must have a balance. The game has changed since the 1960s and you have to change with it. Tottenham didn't have to prove anything to me and there is talent in the squad, no doubt about it. There was only one club I would have left Southampton for and that was Tottenham.

'They are lovely people down there and I've loved working with the Southampton players, but the option came up and I said "yes". It has taken time, but all that is behind us now and I'm looking forward to Sunday's match.'

With a new manager installed, Ledley was left to nurse his dead leg and concentrate on getting himself fit for the Arsenal game at Old Trafford. 'I think I should be all right,' he said in the build-up. 'I've been having a bit of treatment, but I'm training. I was close to playing at Highbury, I was in the squad, but it was decided in the morning that it was best to leave it for that game... The main priority is Sunday and I didn't want to do any further damage to myself.'

Fortunately, Spurs' cautious attitude to the 20-year-old's fitness was to pay dividends and he was declared fit, but his dreams of starting the game were dashed when Hoddle decided to overhaul the team's formation and opted to line up 3-4-3. Sol Campbell, Gary Doherty and Chris Perry were the back three and Ledley was consigned to the bench.

The game in Manchester was as fiercely contested as everyone had predicted and it was Tottenham who got their noses in front in the 14th minute when Doherty headed past David Seaman in the Arsenal goal. Spurs had taken a tentative step towards the Final and it seemed Hoddle's messianic return was going to prove the catalyst for a revival.

But Arsenal equalised nineteen minutes later through Patrick Vieira, then disaster struck in the 38th minute when Sol Campbell was involved in a tussle with Ray Parlour. Campbell had been an injury doubt before the game and soon, as he disentangled himself from the midfielder, it was obvious he was in serious trouble. His suspect ankle had gone again and Hoddle immediately ordered Ledley to warm up. He was to get his chance to shine in the semi-final after all and, as Campbell was stretchered off, Ledley strode purposefully out on to the Old Trafford turf.

Half-time came and went and, after the break, Spurs found themselves under siege as the Gunners pressed for the winner. It was all hands to the pump and, however resolute Ledley and Co were in their efforts to keep them out, it was inevitable that the dam would eventually be breached and it was Robert Pires who delivered the killer blow 15 minutes from time. The FA Cup dream was over for another season.

'I don't think we played well enough to win,' Hoddle conceded after the game. 'We were a bit negative in our passing and I think they can pass better than that. That's where we let ourselves down – we weren't big enough and strong enough mentally on the ball. We need to pass the ball better and that's one thing we have to look to improve.'

With the team languishing in the bottom half of the table, the season was effectively over and it was time for Hoddle to run the rule over his new charges in the remaining games of the campaign. Ledley was rested for the next fixture at home to Bradford but was recalled to the starting line-up for the trip to Wearside to face Sunderland four days later. There may have been little to play for in terms of the league but, for Ledley, it was an opportunity to demonstrate his mettle to the new manager. Speculation about possible summer transfer targets was rife and, with

Hoddle already rumoured to be pressing for a move for Dean Richards, his defensive rock at Southampton, it was imperative that the youngster made an impression.

The Stadium of Light clash was to prove painful for Ledley in more ways than one. Initially, there was the indignity of Sunderland scoring twice in the opening twelve minutes, but far worse was to follow. In the nineteenth minute, he suffered a sickening clash of heads with Kevin Kilbane and his match was over.

The diagnosis was bleak. He had fractured a cheekbone in the collision and it would require surgery to repair the damage. His injury jinx had struck again and Spurs fans would have to wait until the following season to see him in action once more.

The operation, at least, went well. The damage was repaired swiftly, clearing the way for what he hoped would be an injury-free pre-season later that summer. 'I had the operation and they lifted the bone up,' he revealed to the club website after he was discharged from hospital. 'It's about healing at the moment and I'll probably be out of action for about four or five weeks. They actually went through the top of my head, went in and lifted the bone up, but it actually looks worse than it is... it's not too bad.

'It was a collision. I don't remember too much about it, but it must have been quite a big bang. I'm not too bad at the moment, though. I had the operation, then rested for a week and I can do a bit of running in the next week or two, so I'll be doing that to keep my fitness up. I've been doing a bit of weights and on the bike and stuff.'

Without his athletic services, Spurs limped home over

the finishing line with three further defeats, a draw and a 3–1 victory over Manchester United at the Lane in the final fixture of the season. The team had finished in a lowly 12th place.

It had been a tumultuous nine months for the club. New owners and a new manager had been installed over the course of the season and although few, if any, fans were happy with the mid-table finish, there was a sense that the fundamental changes that had taken place were for the better. Few mourned the departure of Sir Alan Sugar as chairman and the return of Hoddle to his spiritual home felt like the final piece of the jigsaw. The new season was suddenly full of promise.

For Ledley, it was a year of contrasts. The agony of missing the start of the campaign through injury was quickly forgotten as he slowly began to establish himself in the first team – playing 25 times in league and Cup – and his quick fire début goal against Bradford ensured him a place in the record books. He had also forged a successful England Under-21 career and enjoyed the experience of an FA Cup run, even though the team had fallen at the penultimate hurdle.

There were many positives for the 20-year-old to glean from what was effectively his début season of first-team action. His sickening injury at Sunderland may have ended his involvement prematurely, but there was no doubt he was a genuine star in the making.

The controversial events of the summer of 2001 that rocked Spurs to its foundations were only to accelerate Ledley's meteoric rise to the very top.

3

THE MAIN MAN

When Sol Campbell joined Tottenham as an aspiring trainee in 1989, few could have predicted the enormous impact he would go on to have at the club. The Plaistow-born centre-half certainly had talent and all the prerequisite physical attributes to forge a successful top-flight career for himself, but in a twelve-year love affair with Spurs, he was to become so much more than merely a first-team star.

In short, Campbell grew to become the heart and soul of the club. In a period when the fans were starved of success and silverware, he was the standard bearer, the shining light and the terrace icon. He was homegrown, he was indisputably world-class and he belonged to Spurs. The fans worshipped him.

And then it all turned sour. As the 2000/01 season drew

to a close and the rest of the Tottenham squad decamped en masse for their summer holidays, Campbell's future with the club was uncertain. His contract expired at the start of July and, despite the board's repeated efforts to get him to sign a new deal, he had refused to put pen to paper. The White Hart Lane faithful prayed he would have a change of heart but the writing seemed to be on the wall. Sol was leaving the club.

The newspapers were awash with rumours and reports about the various suitors for his services. European giants Barcelona, Inter Milan, Real Madrid and Bayern Munich, as well as Liverpool, all reportedly wanted to sign the England man on a Bosman free transfer and, as July and the end of his contract approached, the speculation reached fever pitch.

And then, just three days after he became a free agent, the startling truth emerged. Campbell had agreed to cross the north London divide and sign for bitter rivals Arsenal. The football world, let alone Spurs fans, were stunned and, once the incredulity had faded, the anger surfaced.

'I've made my decision and I just hope people respect it,' Campbell said in a vain effort to deflect the worst of the criticism when he was unveiled as an Arsenal player. 'Obviously, I know what happened to George Graham when he joined Spurs and what he had to deal with. It is something I am prepared to face and, hopefully, it won't be a major problem for me. I spent a lot of years at Tottenham and, while I was there, I played my heart out and tried everything to help move the team in the right direction. But the time finally came to make a decision to move on.'

He added that he was very keen to stay in the Premiership, even though he could have earned more money abroad. He also admitted that the decision was made with his England career very much at the forefront of his mind.

Campbell's move remains one of the most controversial transfers in recent football history but, more pressingly at the time for Spurs and Glenn Hoddle, it created a yawning hole in the centre of the defence and also left the supporters in urgent need of a new hero, a player nurtured through the club's junior ranks whom they felt they could call their own.

Step forward Ledley Brenton King.

Of course, the comparisons between the two men had been obvious even before Campbell's acrimonious departure. Both were London-born, both had served their apprenticeship in the junior and then reserve teams and both were players the Spurs crowd felt a real sense of affinity with.

Physically, they were also similar. Tall, muscular and yet incredibly athletic, both possessed a deceptive turn of pace and both had forged reputations as fearsome, fearless competitors. In truth, Campbell was arguably stronger in the air than his erstwhile team-mate but Ledley equally was regarded by most as the better in possession. Aside from the six-year age gap, they were almost but not quite two peas in a pod.

It was only natural, then, even before the new season began, that the fans and the media were looking at Ledley as the heir apparent to Campbell's throne. Even David

Pleat, the club's director of football, had unwittingly added to the perception in an interview after Campbell's transfer when he said, 'The king is dead... long live the king.' An innocent slip of the tongue perhaps, but it was what everyone was thinking. It seemed to matter little that the 20-year-old had only had 22 Premiership appearances to his name.

Ledley himself, however, readily admitted to having mixed feelings about Campbell's exit. On the one hand, one of his mentors and closest friends at the club had suddenly vanished, but on the other, it was to thrust him into the spotlight and accelerate his development as senior player.

'When Sol left to sign for Arsenal, I was as upset as anyone because he is such a great player,' he told the *News of the World* two months after Campbell's departure. 'But when he went, it opened the door for me to play at the back. As long as he was at Spurs, I knew I would have to play out of position.

'Sol was already in the first team when I started to go there as a kid and I looked up to him as my hero. He would always have time for a friendly chat and I learned a lot from just watching him. Like him, I worked my way through the junior and reserve teams and when I broke into the first-team squad, he would always be there to encourage me and offer valuable advice. Sometimes we would stay out together after training and work on our touch.'

But before Ledley could worry about shouldering the mantle of the 'new Campbell', he had to focus on his pre-season regime. His broken foot on Under-21 duty at the end of the previous season had denied him priceless time on the training pitch and he was determined not to miss out a second time around. The squad flew out to La Manga in Spain to prepare thoroughly for the new campaign and Ledley relished the opportunity to prepare properly.

'I enjoyed La Manga. The weather was nice but we worked hard. Three sessions a day was quite a lot but it was nice to be out there for pre-season,' he said when the team arrived back in London for a series of pre-season friendlies. 'I think the warm weather does help... it's good when you're training in the heat and I think everyone enjoyed it.'

Ledley's first appearance in the pre-season warm-ups came in a 2–0 win at Reading's Madejski Stadium. It was a routine run-out but, more significantly, Glenn Hoddle took the opportunity in his post-match interview to share his views publicly on the 20-year-old for the first time.

'He missed five days training, so he's been a little bit behind and then he had a couple of days training before the Wycombe game,' Hoddle admitted. 'I was going to play him in the reserves, but I thought, no, we can't wait and wait and wait, the injury wasn't going to be a problem. These are all the things you have to assess as a manager and we gave him the 90 minutes. He played very, very well for a youngster but he made one mistake that could have cost us the win – and that's something he's got to learn from.

'I was delighted with his overall performance and he can learn from that because it was a pre-season game and it's not going to hurt you if he learns from mistakes in a game like that. I think we've got a lot of punch in midfield, a lot of opportunities for people to put pressure on each other. I know Ledley can play in midfield. I haven't worked with him in midfield and, at the moment, I'm looking at the situation at the back.'

The new manager was evidently an admirer, if not an uncritical one. More interestingly, he seemed to envisage Ledley's future at the heart of the Spurs defence.

The new season was to start in mid-August with Aston Villa at White Hart Lane but, before the Premiership bandwagon was up and running once again, Ledley was called up to play for the England Under-21s against Holland. The Under-21s now had a new coach in David Platt and it was a ringing endorsement of the player's qualities that Platt was willing to select him despite his injury problems and his relative inexperience.

It would have been his eighth cap for the side but, in the end, he never actually made it on to the pitch. He picked up a minor ankle strain in a pre-season friendly against Greek side AEK Athens and, rather than risk him on the eve of the new season, Ledley was allowed to rest and recuperate.

The decision meant that he was fighting fit for the Villa game but, despite his earlier assertions that he saw Ledley as a natural centre-back, Hoddle played him in the Tottenham midfield. The match was instantly forgettable, however, and a goalless draw was a fair reflection of the uninspiring performance from both sides. The season opener had failed to provide the anticipated pyrotechnics.

A few days later, the newspapers were full of the story that Hoddle was poised to lure centre-half Dean Richards to the Lane from his old club Southampton. If true, the deal could represent a blow to King's aspirations to play regularly in the back four and, after the manager's insistence on deploying him in midfield against Villa, there was renewed doubt about exactly where on the pitch his future lay.

'The competition for places is good within the squad but, if someone new does come in, I'll be working hard to impress further and we'll see what happens,' Ledley said in an interview when pressed for his views on the Richards story. 'I know I'm only young but I'd like to stay in the side for as many games as I can. I don't want to be a bit part player now. I will always fight for my shirt and I see this season as the one in which I will cement my place in the first team. I feel I can do really well given the chance.'

On the same day as Ledley's resolute pronouncements were taken up by the media, Hoddle was also cornered by the press. He admitted that he was indeed looking to bring in defensive reinforcements but he also sent an encouraging message to his young star-in-the-making. 'I am trying to strengthen the defence with another signing but, if Ledley keeps on putting in the performances, he will do well,' Hoddle said. 'We looked at him during pre-season and he played solidly for us. He is comfortable on both sides of the pitch and he's got a lot of talent to work with. He is ahead of Sol Campbell when he was his age but what he hasn't got yet is his pace and presence. But if we can teach him to defend cutely, then he can progress. I think you can let him grow with the team. What you can't do is have three or four doing that or you will get caught at this level. He is not the finished article at the moment but it will be interesting to see where he is in two years.'

Spurs' next fixture was a tricky trip to Goodison to face Everton and Ledley was again part of a midfield quartet until Gary Doherty and Gus Poyet were both sent off in quick succession in the second-half, and Tottenham were forced to mount a valiant rearguard with only nine men. It was ultimately a successful operation and Hoddle's side clung on for a creditable 1–1 draw.

Defeat at Blackburn and victory over Hoddle's former club Southampton ensued before Ledley returned to the Under-21 fold for a vital European Championship qualifier against Germany in Freiburg. It was to be a severe examination of Platt's youngsters and, despite being forced to withdraw from the friendly against Holland at the start of the season, the coach had no hesitation in including Ledley in his starting XI.

The day after the Under-21s game, the senior side were to make their own little bit of history with their famous 5–1 win over Germany at the Olympiastadion in Munich and, in truth, that result all but obscured what was an equally outstanding performance from the next generation of England stars.

The Germans were confident of victory over Platt's team but goals from Joe Cole and Francis Jeffers earned England a magnificent 2–1 victory. The senior team may have won in their friendly outing, but the Under-21s had done the business in a qualifier and Ledley, in the heart of the defence, had more than played his part.

Buoyed by their triumph, the Under-21s prepared for their second qualifier in five days. This time they had home advantage in the shape of Middlesbrough's Riverside Stadium and the opposition – Albania – were unlikely to give the players sleepless nights.

It proved to be the stroll that everyone anticipated. England scored five, while Ledley and his fellow defenders had one of the easiest nights of their relatively short careers. The international break had yielded two contrasting but equally welcome victories.

'The pleasing thing was the maturity of the performance and the fact we maintained it for the entire 90 minutes,' Platt said after his side his side's Riverside romp. 'Sometimes, when you go two or three goals up, players can start showboating, but these boys kept it going right to the end. They maintained their professionalism to the final whistle. Ledley King was magnificent at the back.

'Albania were a little more attack-minded than I thought they would be after having a good win against Finland, but they still got plenty of people behind the ball and we had to combat that. You have to trust in what you believe and we knew if we could spread them out they would become tired and the space would eventually come, which is what happened.'

Spurs were in League Cup action against Torquay United at White Hart Lane when Ledley returned. It was to be his début in the competition and the Tottenham fans thronged through the turnstiles in anticipation of a handsome victory against the sacrificial lambs from the lower league.

But as so often transpires in such David and Goliath encounters, Torquay played out of their skins and, with an hour gone, Spurs had still not found a way through. The crowd were becoming increasingly restless and a potentially embarrassing result suddenly seemed to be a possibility... until Ledley took control.

German midfielder Christian Ziege curled an inviting left-footed free-kick into the box and Ledley was in exactly the right place at the right time to steer the ball deftly in from close range. Spurs, not to mention the crowd, visibly relaxed as the ball hit the back of the net and Les Ferdinand added a degree of gloss to the final scoreline eight minutes later with the second. It had not been a vintage performance against plucky opposition but they were through.

Eight days later, Spurs signed Richards from Southampton as had been widely predicted in the papers. The deal cost the club more than £8 million and, at that price, it was obvious the new recruit was going to be brought straight into the first team sooner rather than later. Ledley had new (and expensive) competition for the centre-half berth.

The transfer went through too late for Richards to be included in the Spurs squad to face Liverpool at Anfield the following day, so Ledley partnered Chris Perry in central defence. The duo were magnificent on Merseyside and it took a moment of sublime magic from Liverpool's

Finnish striker Jari Litmanen to break the deadlock. It was the only goal of the game and Spurs knew their battling performance should have been rewarded with a share of the points. More significantly, both Ledley and Perry put down their markers. Neither player was about to surrender their place in the back four without a fight.

Perhaps mindful of the potential impact the Richards signing had had on his England Under-21 star, Hoddle came out and reiterated his confidence in the player after his Anfield display and there was no mention of his midfield attributes. 'He's got a rare talent in that he's an English defender who can play off both feet,' the manager told the *Daily Telegraph*. 'He's impressed me immensely. He's come in this season and been our most consistent player and he looks as if he can get better and better. He's quick, deceptively so, and big and physically strong, so he's got every attribute a defender needs. We've just got to make sure he doesn't take his foot off the pedal and he keeps working on his concentration – that's where youngsters get found out. But with experience and confidence, there's no limit to what he can achieve.'

'My only criticism would be Ledley's probably too quiet. I want him to be more demonstrative, to boss people about on the pitch. But the good thing about Ledley is that he is a level-headed lad who learns quickly.'

The defeat to Liverpool meant Spurs had won just two of their opening seven Premiership games. It was not a full-blown crisis but Hoddle's honeymoon period had already clearly come and gone and the need for a run of results was becoming more pressing. The Spurs faithful were not going to turn on their prodigal son at this early stage, but the pressure was growing.

Unfortunately, the next game was the visit of defending champions Manchester United to the Lane. It was a tough assignment for a side in search of a morale-boosting victory. Hoddle handed Richards his début and, in fairytale style, the big defender marked it with the opening goal of the match after just 15 minutes. The 36,000-strong crowd went wild and Spurs sensed there could be an upset on the cards. The expectation reached fever pitch ten minutes later when Les Ferdinand doubled Tottenham's lead after he beat the offside trap and drilled the ball clinically past the United goalkeeper Fabien Barthez.

The majority of the home fans would have gladly settled for a two-goal lead at half-time but, just before the break, it was three as Christian Ziege found the back of the net with a powerful, diving header. White Hart Lane was simultaneously overcome with a sense of disbelief and a rush of adrenalin.

Spurs knew they would have endure a second-half onslaught from the champions, who doubtless had to suffer a frank and vocal assessment of their performance from Alex Ferguson, and it was vital they weathered the initial storm.

And when the storm came, Tottenham buckled. Andy Cole pulled one back for United within two minutes of the restart and Spurs were clearly nervous. Further goals from Laurent Blanc, Ruud van Nistelrooy, Juan Verón and David Beckham followed without reply and a three-goal lead had dramatically been transformed into a 5–3 defeat. Ledley and the rest of the team trooped dejectedly off the pitch in stunned silence.

It was an experience that had a profound effect on all the players. The Jekyll and Hyde performance encapsulated the best and worst of Tottenham under Hoddle and, even years later, Ledley admitted it was painful to remember the days' events. 'We went into a half-time lead and didn't really want the break to come,' he said. 'We sat down and talked about how United would come at us and not to panic. Unfortunately, they scored straight away and it all went wrong from there. I have the video at home but haven't watched it. It's a game I would like to forget.'

As the dust settled on the capitulation, Ledley joined up once again with the England Under-21 squad for a European Championship qualifier against Greece at Blackburn. It was his tenth cap but there was by now the growing feeling that he was ready to make the step up to the senior side. He would turn 21 exactly a week after the Greece game and his performances for the Under-21s had already proved he had the qualities to play international football. Sol Campbell and Manchester United's Rio Ferdinand were Sven-Göran Eriksson's first-choice central defence pairing, but Ledley was pushing them hard now. It was only a matter of time before his chance would come.

The Greece game only confirmed his credentials. England took an early lead through Jermain Defoe and went in at half-time one goal to the good. The second-half, however, was a different story as the Greeks lay siege to the England goal and, without a series of outstanding interventions from Ledley, the visitors would have equalised. England doubled their advantage late on and, although the Spurs man did give away a 90th-minute penalty after a debatable foul on Giannis Papadopoulis, which the striker converted, the real work had already been done and England were 2–1 winners.

Ledley went on to play two more games for the Under-21s. They were his final appearances for the side and proved to be a fitting epitaph to his England career at junior level. The matches were a home and away clash with Holland in November in a winner-takes-all play-off for a place in the European Championship finals in the summer.

The first leg in Utrecht saw Ledley and central defensive partner John Terry facing one of the toughest tests of their short careers as the inventive and skilful Dutch forwards probed the England back four and, despite some desperate last-ditch tackles, the home side surged into a two-goal lead with future Liverpool striker Dirk Kuyt helping himself to Holland's second. To their credit, England refused to buckle and, on the stroke of half-time, gave themselves a lifeline when midfielder Sean Davis, who was briefly to play alongside Ledley at Spurs less than three years later, fired in a superb near-post header. England had given themselves a chance.

The second half saw many flowing Dutch attacks but, this time, Ledley and Terry stood firm and there was no way through. At the other end, captain David Dunn was evidently relishing the burden of leadership and, when he picked up the ball inside the Dutch half on the hour, it was obvious he fancied his chances. The Blackburn midfielder beat one man, then another, a third and then a fourth, before finding the back of the net to put his side on level terms. There were no more goals on a cold, crisp night in Utrecht and England flew home in high spirits to prepare for the return match.

'It was some comeback but, when you're 2–0 down, you have to produce one,' Platt said after the final whistle. 'I thought in the first half we were probably guilty of believing in each other a bit too much. I don't think we ever got going really in the first half but full credit to them because at 2–0 down in international football, you can go under, especially away from home. But it's only half-time now and we have to finish the job off at Pride Park.'

The match was at Derby and turned out to be a complete contrast to the fluid, open first leg in Holland. Both sides sensed the winning line and tightened up as result and, in the end, it was a solitary goal from midfielder Michael Carrick, another future White Hart Lane star, who broke the deadlock on 72 minutes, scrappily poking the ball home from close range. England were 1–0 winners and on their way to the finals.

After his series of commanding and combative performances for Platt's side, there was already speculation that Ledley might be heading east for the World Cup with the senior squad rather than rejoining the Under-21s for their European adventure. Of course, the man himself refused to get carried away with the hype, but it was telling that he already had to deflect the questions about his summer plans. 'One or the other tournament will be very, very nice,' he told the club website. 'If I don't make it to the World Cup – and I'm not putting any pressure on myself to do that – then hopefully I'll be with the Under-21s. I'll look forward to either.

'I remember well playing in the last Under-21 European Championship finals in Slovakia. It was the first time I'd played in a big tournament like that and I was only nineteen. I didn't have any Premiership experience then, but I have now and I'll go into the next tournament with all the more confidence because of that.

'It's great news for everyone that we made the finals. It gives players the chance to face different teams and different players, styles of football that they don't come up against every day. It will help everyone's progress.'

Back at White Hart Lane, it was obvious the Spurs squad were still smarting after their United mauling and the fans waited with bated breath to see what psychological effect the result would have on the players. Would they be stung into action by the very public humiliation or would they take longer to recover from events at White Hart Lane?

Fortunately for the team, and Ledley, the former reaction turned out to be the case. In the next nine league and Cup games, Tottenham were beaten just once – a 2–1 defeat to Leeds at Elland Road – and, by the start of December, it felt as though the wound had finally healed. The Hoddle feelgood factor was in full flow and the side were heading in the right direction in the Premiership.

The busy Christmas period loomed and Spurs were looking in fine fettle, earning widespread praise for their attacking brand of football and, most importantly, picking up league points on a consistent basis.

'The manager has brought in five or six top-class players and that has shone through the team,' Ledley said when asked to explain the team's impressive resurgence. 'Their quality is helping to bring the best out of the youngsters at the club and the competition is so fierce, that's another thing.'

Tottenham's rapidly rising star also pointed out that the team was buzzing, and the feeling of achieving more and more that season was infectious, with everyone wanting a piece of the action. Having thought that the team might take a couple of seasons to gel, now there was real belief that success was a tangible reality, and that current form might yield a European qualifying position. Ledley insisted that that was what everyone was focusing on.

At the same time, it was obvious that Ledley was beginning to feel more comfortable with his status as a first-team regular. When fit, he was now an automatic choice in the side and, although he had lost a little of his innate modesty and mastery of the understatement, it was clear he was thriving under the managerial regime at the club.

'As soon as Glenn clapped eyes on me, he switched me to defence,' he told the *Sunday Mirror*. 'Glenn and John Gorman have worked tirelessly to iron out any faults in my game. They felt I had the potential to play at the back and worked with me before, during and after training.

Defence is a home from home to me. He encourages me to express myself on the ball.

'When I look at myself on videos, I look lazy, slow and sluggish. But that is just the way I play. I look laid-back even when I'm not trying to. My pace is decent, I'm quite strong and I'm decent on the ball. My heading is still not up to scratch.'

Boxing Day 2001 saw Spurs travel to the south coast to play Southampton, Hoddle's former club, but the match did not only hold a special significance for the Tottenham manager alone. For the 21-year-old Ledley, it was to be his 50th senior appearance for the club and, although the occasion was not exactly back-page news, it nonetheless represented another milestone in his career.

Sadly, the match failed to give Ledley cause for much post-match celebration. The Saints team and the crowd were still bitter that Hoddle had left them to take the Tottenham job and the atmosphere at St Mary's was extremely hostile. The Southampton players fed off the vitriol directed at Hoddle and his side and emerged 1–0 winners, thanks to James Beattie's second-half header.

It was a blow to Spurs but they quickly shrugged off the disappointment to take four points from a possible six in their next two outings against Aston Villa and Blackburn to prove their recent run of form had not merely been a flash in the pan.

Ledley's own form continued to impress. The Spurs fans already knew all about their new hero but, with every game, he was earning plaudits and rave reviews from further afield. He still hadn't even featured in the senior England squad, let alone made his full début, but speculation that he would be a member of the World Cup squad was growing. Even Dean Richards, the man brought in by Hoddle to strengthen the Tottenham defence, felt compelled to add his voice to the chorus of King admirers. 'I think he's capable of making the World Cup squad,' Richards said. 'If he plays the way he's played so far, continuing that consistency and how he's played for the Under-21s as well, I can't see a reason why he can't squeeze into the squad. And if not this one, he'll be involved in the next one, definitely.' Richards said that he'd played against Ledley a couple of times, and now having partnered him as well, he was sure that the Tottenham hero would go on to become one of England's greatest defenders. Interestingly, Richards also mentioned that he'd been helping Ledley with one aspect of his game in particular – communication with the other players – and felt that he was improving all the time.

Now in the depths of January, the team were scheduled to face Chelsea in the semi-final of the League Cup. It was an eagerly-anticipated London derby, not least because Tottenham had not beaten their city rivals in any competition for twelve long years (or 25 games) and a place in the Final at Cardiff's Millennium Stadium awaited the winner over the two legs.

The first game was at Stamford Bridge and there was a frenzied atmosphere when the two sides emerged from the tunnel. Chelsea were the favourites but Spurs had enjoyed a run of form that suggested they were capable of finally ending their dismal record against the Blues. The home side struck first, though, when Kasey Keller was unable to prevent a Jimmy Floyd Hasselbaink effort squirming under his body after ten minutes with Tottenham already having their backs to the wall. The two teams went into the break with no further score, but Spurs came out for the second half looking the more purposeful, and they were back on level terms when Les Ferdinand beat the offside trap yet again and, this time, made the most of his opportunity to bring Spurs back on level terms.

The pace of the game remained fast and furious, but it was Chelsea who enjoyed a large slice of luck seconds before scoring what was to be the winning goal. Ledley was harshly adjudged to have handled the ball by referee Alan Riley when it appeared to the majority watching in the ground that it was Hasselbaink's hand that had made contact. Riley awarded Chelsea a debatable free-kick. Initially, there seemed no immediate danger because the ball was still 30 yards from Keller's goal, but Hasselbaink stepped forward to lash the dead ball straight through the wall and past Keller, giving him no chance. Chelsea's hoodoo over Spurs had struck again and Hoddle's side would have to overturn a 2–1 deficit in the second leg if they were to reach the Final. 'That free-kick was a decision that really hurt us,' Hoddle fumed after the game. 'It was a key decision. For me, it's a simple decision they should get right, but I've got to say I thought there was a possibility there could have been a penalty against us as well. That was a tougher decision.'

There was little time for Spurs to reflect on their sense of injustice and they were on the road three days later to face Ipswich at Portman Road. Perhaps the side were still thinking of what might have been at Stamford Bridge because they produced an inauspicious performance and were beaten 2–1. Ipswich scored with two free headers and fingers were immediately pointed at the Tottenham defence. Lesser players may have tried to avoid the match post mortem in such circumstances but Ledley refused to slip away without facing the media.

'Personally, I was disappointed with my marking for the first goal,' he admitted. 'The second one came off me... We're disappointed to concede two goals from corners and we'll be making sure that doesn't happen again. Mistakes do happen, of course they do. It's about learning from them, picking them out and making sure they don't happen too often.

'We've got three crucial games coming up, starting off with the FA Cup against Coventry and then the return leg against Chelsea and we're looking forward to both – these are exciting times for us.'

The Coventry game was a third-round clash at Highfield Road in mid-January. The match was a repeat of the famous 1987 Final in which the Sky Blues triumphed 3–2, so, in an effort to evoke the memories of the most famous day in the club's history, Coventry paraded the winning team on the pitch before kick-off. The 2002 rematch, however, was an altogether more one-sided affair.

Tottenham were into their stride from the start and their slick, passing football meant it was only a matter of time before they made the breakthrough. It came courtesy of Gus Poyet midway through the first half and when Les Ferdinand added the second minutes after the break, the result was beyond doubt.

Ledley sat out the next game – a Premiership stalemate with Everton at White Hart Lane – to ensure he was fit for the Chelsea showdown. It was the first match of the campaign in which he had not featured and Hoddle's decision to name him on the bench even though he had no injury problems reflected his importance to the team. The 21-year-old was now one of the first names on the team sheet and it was unthinkable for Spurs to go into the biggest game of the season without his services.

'It's a tough one but we've played them twice and I believe we deserved something out of the games on both occasions, so we're not frightened of them in any way,' he told the club website. 'We're at home and we'll be looking to impose our football on them. We will look to defend properly, keep a clean sheet and we'll have to be on the top of our game to keep the front two quiet. Hasselbaink and Gudjohnsen work together well, even though they are quite similar, so that's unusual. They drop off together, play close and you have to remain sharp all the time. We will have to stay switched on.

'To play in a final is something you want to do when you are young... you watch them on television and hope one day you might get there yourself. We're one game away at the moment. There are a lot of young players in the squad and it would be a great achievement.'

The White Hart Lane crowd were in expectant mood when the two sides trooped out but surely not even the most optimistic Tottenham fan could have envisaged the dramatic events that were to unfold over the next 90 minutes. Ledley had spoken in the build-up of the danger of pushing too hard for the all-important goal too early in the encounter but such a pragmatic approach seemed to be abandoned as soon as the first whistle blew. In fact, there were a mere 105 seconds on the clock when Spurs scored their first. Argentinian full-back Mauricio Taricco saw his shot parried by Chelsea 'keeper Carlo Cudicini but John Terry hesitated with his clearance and striker Steffen Iversen bundled home the ball in his first start for the club in six months. Tottenham were one up with less than two minutes played. It was a dream start and levelled the tie at 2–2 on aggregate, but Spurs were in no mood to rely on the away-goal rule to see them through to the Final.

The second came on 33 minutes and was a joy to behold. Darren Anderton delivered a low, driven corner. Tim Sherwood escaped his marker, spun on a sixpence and unleashed a fizzing shot that almost burst Cudicini's net. Tottenham were on fire and Chelsea were praying for the half-time whistle.

But there was to be no respite for the visitors after the break. Skipper Teddy Sheringham had missed the first leg at Stamford Bridge through injury but marked his return to the team in the 50th minute, latching on to Gus Poyet's chest-down and volleying crisply into the far corner. Three-nil to Spurs with half-an-hour to play.

Chelsea were by now growing increasingly desperate and their frustration boiled over when Hasselbaink slapped Sheringham in the face. In a case of mistaken identity, referee Mark Halsey actually sent off Blues defender Mario Melchiot but, whoever the culprit, Chelsea were reduced to ten men and facing a vibrant home side intent on adding insult to injury.

Three became four with fifteen minutes to play when Welsh international Simon Davies beat Cudicini at the near post and the rout was completed late on when substitute Sergei Rebrov netted from close range after just four minutes on the pitch. Chelsea grabbed a meaningless consolation goal in the 90th minute but it did nothing to disguise the extent of their humiliation. Tottenham were heading to the Final in the most convincing style possible.

'We couldn't have asked for a better performance,' Hoddle said after beating one of his former clubs and ending Spurs' twelve-year jinx against their London rivals. 'Our finishing was clinical, our passing and movement and also the way the back three defended was superb. To score five goals was magnificent and it could have been more.

'Five different goalscorers says it all and that was after we lost our leading goalscorer, Les Ferdinand, before kick-off. I'm delighted for everyone at the club, the fans, because it's been a hard time for them with this record against Chelsea, but that's evened it up for them in one fell swoop. The crowd were fantastic. They knew what a big night it was and they've been entertained along the way.'

The reward for their Chelsea demolition job was a Final against Blackburn Rovers in Cardiff. It would be the first major club final of Ledley's career but, before he could look forward to gracing the big stage, Spurs were back in Cup action, this time in the fourth round of the FA Cup against Bolton at the Lane. Hoddle's side had routed Wanderers 6–0 in the League Cup and there were high expectations of a repeat performance.

The fans were not disappointed. Although Hoddle rested Sheringham, Ferdinand and Chris Perry to avoid the danger of them picking up a yellow card and being suspended for the League Cup Final, Spurs were once again in rampant form in and scored four unanswered goals to continue their recent prolific form. Darren Anderton's 22nd-minute penalty got the ball rolling and Tottenham scored almost at will after that. There could have been a repeat of the earlier 6–0 trouncing but for the heroics of the Bolton 'keeper, Jussi Jaaskelainen, and with just one Premiership fixture between the team and the big game in Cardiff, Spurs were in fine fettle.

It was the best period of Ledley's career to date. His own performances were improving with each game, his manager had publicly (and repeatedly) declared him the lynchpin of his defence and the team were playing well, particularly in the Cups. He had already suffered more than his fair share of injury setbacks for such a young player but he was now a model of consistency in a vibrant, confident side.

If he thought things couldn't get much better, he was sorely mistaken. Just five days after Bolton were mercilessly pulled apart, Ledley received the news that he had yearned to hear ever since he began kicking the ball around with his mates in The Cage. Sven-Göran Eriksson had announced his squad for a friendly with the Dutch in Amsterdam and the name of Ledley Brenton King was on the all-important list. The boy from Bow was to be a part of the full England set-up.

There are countless tales of talented young footballers who have played for England Under-16s, the Under-18s, even the Under-21s, and yet still never fulfilled their dream of pulling on the famous white shirt for the senior team. Like many others before him, Ledley had graduated through the FA ranks with the ambition to make it all the way to the top and Eriksson's decision to promote him from the Under-21s represented the final leg of the journey. The Holland match was a friendly, a chance for the respective managers to look at new players and try new combinations, and it was widely accepted that Ledley would play. He wasn't joining the squad just to make up the numbers.

'I saw Ledley play a few times last season and he was playing well then but this season I think he is playing even better,' Eriksson told the media at the announcement of his squad. 'He is big, strong and good on the ball, too.'

It was left to Hoddle, one of Eriksson's predecessors in the England job, to paint a fuller picture of the player's meteoric progress and the reasons why he was on the verge of his first full cap. 'It is great for the club and great for Ledley, especially in a World Cup year, and I am absolutely delighted for him,' Hoddle said. 'Ledley has impressed me immensely with his level of consistency this season – nothing seems to faze him. He has been absolutely marvellous. The potential is there, and where he can go in the future is in his own hands, and those of the people he is working with. He is everything I hoped for, but probably two years earlier than I thought we would have him, so I am delighted with him and with the way he is playing. I didn't get much of a chance to work with him last season because he fractured his cheekbone soon after I came in. When I arrived here, Ledley was a midfield player... but I didn't see him as a midfield player.'

Hoddle added that he saw Ledley as an obvious defender, and that his performances so far had proved the truth of that. Ledley was, as far as Hoddle was concerned, highly adaptable, but particularly strong at the back – he could win balls in the air, he had pace, he was strong and two-footed – all attributes which, if combined with a maturing psychological approach, could take him all the way to becoming one of the best defenders in England. Again, two areas that Hoddle identified as being areas for development were Ledley's talking and concentration. Those could be learned – the natural ability Ledley displayed on the pitch was already there in spades.

The player himself was modesty personified when the news of his call-up broke. Calm, cool and collected on the pitch, he was exactly the same off it and it was evident it just didn't matter to him how many glowing reviews he received. Ledley was already not a man to be swayed by others' honeyed words and he reacted to Eriksson's selection with a cautious sense of anticipation. 'As a youngster, it's what you dream of, playing for your country,' he said. 'If I'm lucky enough to do it, that would be great. I've done OK in the last few games and I'll be confident. I always get nervous, so that won't be anything different, but I'll take it all in and try to enjoy it. I'm sure it will be a great experience. All I can do is go out there and play.'

Ledley reported for England duty with former England Under-21 team-mates Darius Vassell, Wayne Bridge, Michael Ricketts and Joe Cole in readiness for the clash in the Amsterdam Arena and, as had widely been predicted, he seemed destined to make the starting line-up. Until, that is, fate intervened and he was forced to pull out of the squad. The 21-year-old had already had to overcome a series of injuries in the previous two years but his heartbreaking departure from the England camp was caused by something as innocuous as a bout of tonsillitis. His dreams of representing his country had been dashed.

'Ledley has tonsillitis,' Hoddle said when asked to explain his player's last-minute withdrawal. 'That was the reason he wasn't involved with England. He's been put on antibiotics and he has to be a doubt for the Final against Blackburn.'

Ledley could have been forgiven for thinking his world had suddenly collapsed around his ears. One minute, he was preparing to run out in England colours for the first time and the next he was on a plane back to England. To compound his misery, he was also faced with the bleak prospect of missing the biggest game of his Spurs career courtesy of a mundane infection.

Inevitably, however, the young man took his misfortune

philosophically and could only see the positives in his recent experience. He also refused to accept he wouldn't be available for the Final against Blackburn. 'I started to feel it on the Monday night, the first day I was away really,' he told the club's website. 'I was trying to battle on with it and hoped it would get better, but it seemed to get worse. I informed the England doctor and I was on some medication, but it didn't get any better and unfortunately I had to pull out. I'm definitely disappointed but these things happen and, hopefully, I'll get another chance. I'm still on antibiotics at the moment. I'll be taking them for the next week or so to make sure it doesn't come back. I should be fit for Sunday. It was my first training session back today [Wednesday] and I don't feel too bad and I'll just carry on working hard until the end of the week.

'It was great to be involved in the England squad; the training was really good and the quality was top class. It was nice just to be around top-quality players.'

Uncharacteristically for someone so usually cautious and considered, Ledley even allowed himself to think ahead to the big match, even though his involvement in Cardiff was far from assured. It was obvious the sense of occasion was even beginning to get to him. 'I think it's going to be a tight game,' he said. 'They are a good side and have got some good players. It'll be tight with not too many goals, like the last game we played. I'm quite confident... But I'm also always nervous before games. I enjoy my nerves, it helps me to prepare. Once I'm on the pitch, the nerves go and I'm just normal.'

Ledley had been due some luck for some time, and the

footballing gods obviously agreed. The antibiotics, not to mention sheer bloody-mindedness, worked their magic and the heart of the Tottenham team was declared fit. His full England cap had been cruelly snatched from him but he would have his chance to sample the atmosphere of a Cup Final after all.

As the two teams took to the pitch in Cardiff, there was a vociferous but also slightly bizarre atmosphere in the Millennium Stadium. The ground's famous roof was closed and this was to be the first Cup Final in the history of the competition to be played 'indoors'.

The early exchanges were predictably fierce as the occasion and the adrenalin pumped up both sets of players. The first real chance of the game fell to Spurs in the 22nd minute when Les Ferdinand latched on to Gus Poyet's inviting through ball, beat the offside trap and then appeared to have rounded Rovers 'keeper Brad Friedel, only for the American to throw out a despairing hand and tip Ferdinand's shot around the post.

Spurs were the side posing more questions but Blackburn hit them on the break midway through the first half to take the lead against the run of play. Keith Gillespie hit a long-range shot more in hope than in expectation but his effort took a deflection off Ben Thatcher en route and into the path of striker Matt Jansen, who crashed an effort under the body of Neil Sullivan and into the back of the net. Tottenham were going to have to come from behind if they were to lift the trophy.

The lead lasted just eight minutes. Again, the vision of

Poyet in midfield was the catalyst and, again, it was Ferdinand's pace and power that took him past the Blackburn defence towards Friedel's goal. But this time, rather than risk the shot from a tight angle, the striker cut back inside, beat two bemused defenders and picked out Christian Ziege at the far post with a perfect pass. The German kept his cool, steered the ball home and the two teams were all square.

By now, chances were coming at both ends with crowd-pleasing regularity but it wasn't until the second half that there was another gilt-edged opportunity. Poyet found himself in the clear and stormed towards goal and fired in a powerful shot that Friedel could only stand and watch. Agonisingly for Spurs, however, the effort smashed into the angle of the upright and crossbar and flew back out.

Up until now, Ledley had marshalled the Spurs defence with his trademark coolness and muscular presence despite it being an open game, which didn't favour the defenders. But in the 69th minute, disaster struck as Blackburn pushed for a second and, for a split-second, Ledley wasn't at his imperious best. Rovers pumped the ball into the box and indecision suddenly gripped the Tottenham defence. Ledley moved in to avert the danger but his header fell invitingly for striker Andy Cole, who accepted his unexpected gift and scooped the ball past Sullivan in the far corner.

It was a cruel twist of fate that it was Ledley's mistake that had led to the goal. Spurs' player of the season so far had been punished for his one lapse in the match and the team only had 20 minutes to repair the damage.

Spurs threw the kitchen sink at Blackburn and, with three minutes left, were denied what seemed a cast-iron penalty when Nils-Eric Johansson felled Teddy Sheringham in the box. The Tottenham players were convinced it was a foul, but referee Graham Poll ignored their desperate appeals for a spot-kick.

There was to be one last chance in the dying seconds when Ferdinand rose above the Rovers defence only to see Friedel gratefully clutching his resulting header rather than picking it out of the back of the net. Blackburn had won their first piece of major silverware in 74 years and Spurs were left to rue what might have been.

The media harshly decided Ferdinand would be Spurs' fall guy for his profligacy in front of goal, but Ledley was acutely aware of his role in the defeat. He was inconsolable after the game and it was left to the manager to conduct the post mortem. 'We are very disappointed,' Hoddle said in the post-match press conference. 'In Cup finals, if you create chances you've got to put them away and, in the end, we haven't. The keeper's won Man of the Match, he's had a great game for them.

'The massive key for us is that, in my opinion, it was a nailed-on penalty for Teddy that we didn't get on the day. Blackburn played well, they gave it everything. We played well at stages of the game but not at our very best. The bottom line is, we've created more chances, better chances, and come off losers. That is bitterly disappointing.'

Hoddle was quick to defend Ferdinand when the inevitable questions about the missed chances started flying, but he was also asked about Ledley and

Blackburn's second goal. His response spoke volumes about his opinion of the player. 'Players make mistakes,' Hoddle said. 'He's only made probably two or three mistakes this season. That is not in a game, in a season – he's been immaculate for us. I might add, he feels he could have done better, but look at the way he played afterwards. He didn't let that affect him and that shows the boy has got the right temperament. In the end, he was as good as anyone in trying to retrieve the game.'

Spurs had a week to regroup after Cardiff and there was still much work to be done. The victory over Bolton had set up a mouth-watering FA Cup quarter-final clash with Chelsea and there was still a chance, albeit it slim, of qualifying for next season's UEFA Cup through the league. Hoddle would have to ensure that the hangover from the trip to Cardiff would not last long.

The team's next run out came against Sunderland at White Hart Lane and, although it was not a vintage performance by any stretch of the imagination, goals from Ferdinand and Poyet were enough to secure the points and go some way to erasing the memories of the Blackburn game.

There were sterner tests to come, not least the trip to Old Trafford to face title-chasing Manchester United four days later. The Red Devils were locked in a battle with Arsenal for top spot in the Premiership and, after the now infamous 5–3 defeat at White Hart Lane earlier in the season, Spurs knew they would have to pull out all the stops in Manchester.

Initially, it seemed a shock was indeed on the cards. The

blustery conditions inside Old Trafford were making it difficult for both teams but Simon Davies, Sheringham and Poyet all went close before David Beckham drew first blood for the home side with a classic counter-attack that he rounded off with his left foot.

The goal seemed visibly to deflate Spurs and the game was over before half-time when they were dealt a controversial double body blow. Another United attack worked space for Paul Scholes, who was held back by full-back Mauricio Taricco and, after a moment of hesitation, referee Mike Riley decided to award a penalty. Replays suggested the initial contact had been made outside the box but Riley had made his decision and the penalty stood. Worse followed when he showed Taricco the red card and, as he trooped dejectedly down the tunnel, Ruud van Nistelrooy scored from the spot. Spurs headed into the dressing room trailing 2–0 and reduced to ten men.

United no doubt had ambitions of surpassing the five goals they put past Spurs at the Lane but, to their credit, Ledley and the rest of the defence stood firm and, although Beckham and van Nistelrooy helped themselves to another goal apiece, the visitors were neither completely overrun nor embarrassed in the second 45 minutes.

But precious league points were still lost, and Hoddle was uncharacteristically outspoken after the game when he was asked to give his views on the Taricco incident.

'It was a diabolical decision,' he argued. 'We will appeal, without any shadow of a doubt, because it was an unjust decision. He was one-and-a-half yards outside the penalty area. It should have been a free-kick and a yellow card. If we can't get those decisions right, where do we go? It's a key decision, because at 1–0 down going into half-time I felt we were very much in the game. People might look in the paper in the morning and, at 4–0, it looks like we got a drubbing, but in the first half we had lots of possession, chances before they scored and I would have taken 1–0 at half-time. We might have got something out of the game, but it was never going to happen after getting Tano sent off and going down to ten men.'

The journey back to London was a long one and gave the side ample time for reflection. They now faced the Cup clash with Chelsea and, with their stuttering Premiership form now making UEFA Cup qualification an increasingly forlorn hope, they knew their only route to Europe would be by winning the FA Cup. They all knew Chelsea were aching for revenge after their 5–1 annihilation at the Lane in January but, for Spurs, it was now make or break.

'We've already had three fantastic matches against Chelsea this season and we have come out with the right result once, so it would be nice to even it up for the campaign,' Teddy Sheringham wrote in his match programme column. 'We know it's going to be a difficult game, but I'm sure it will be a cracking one. Let's hope it ends in our favour.'

It didn't. Chelsea were in no mood to go out of another competition at the hands of their London rivals and, fuelled by the desire to exact their revenge, they tore Spurs apart. William Gallas opened the scoring on 12 minutes and further goals from Eidur Gudjohnsen, Graeme Le Saux and Gudjohnsen again completed the demolition job.

It was a horrible performance from the home side. Dumped out of the FA Cup and languishing in mid-table, Spurs' season was coming apart at the seams. Chelsea rubbed further salt into wound three days later when fate decreed that the two teams faced each other in the Premiership at Stamford Bridge and the Blues dished out another 4–0 mauling.

The team were in dire need of leadership and direction and, even though Ledley was still one of the youngest (and newest) members of the squad, it was the 21-year-old who stuck his head above the parapet to try and gets things in perspective. 'We've definitely taken a big step in the right direction this season and I'm sure that will continue,' he argued. 'Our aim for the season was to get into Europe and we are still aiming for that. You could only say that the season has been positive.' Ledley's view was that the new management had improved things, to the point that the team were playing better football, and that boded well for the future. Several new players still had to gel fully, and that meant a long-term plan, rather than a short-term fix. Pragmatically, Ledley pointed to the fact that dwelling on the defeats of recent weeks was a waste of time – the club had Europe to aim for, and he promised that the team would do all in its power to get maximum points from the remaining league games.

Spurs rallied after their four morale-crushing defeats in succession and ended the run at the end of March against

Fulham at Craven Cottage courtesy of first-half strikes from Sheringham and Poyet. It was a blessed relief after a difficult month and Hoddle and his players now began to focus on the season's remaining seven league fixtures.

For Ledley, however, there was also the outstanding matter of a full England cap. And this time he wasn't going to be denied by illness or injury. His time was coming, and he was determined to grab it with both hands.

4

THE ITALIAN JOB

There are few fixtures on the international calendar that can rival the glamour or sense of history of a match between England and Italy. Two of the game's genuine heavyweights, the football-mad nations first crossed swords back in May 1933 and, ever since their 1–1 draw in Rome that day, games between the Three Lions and the Azzurri have been classic, epic encounters that have never failed to capture the public imagination.

In total, the two teams had met 21 times prior to March 2002, the latest scheduled instalment of their rivalry. The game was to be staged at Leeds United's Elland Road ground and, although it was only a friendly, the match had a huge significance. The World Cup in Japan and South Korea was looming large on the horizon and the inevitable speculation about who would make Sven-

Göran Eriksson's final 23-man squad for the biggest football tournament on earth was already raging. Following the clash with the Italians, England only had three further warm-up games before the finals and the jockeying for places had begun in earnest.

The England manager himself fuelled the debate in the build-up to the game in Leeds when he admitted that he already knew the bulk of his squad and that the number of places up for grabs was limited. 'If you take away the three goalkeepers, then I have space to pick 20 outfield players,' Eriksson said. 'Of those, I would say that I have a good idea of maybe 15, 16 or even 17, but I think for those final three places I will sleep on it until the very last day. Certainly, the door is still open and I think there will be a fight to the end for those places.'

If Ledley was to make a late charge for a World Cup place, it would have to be now. Despite Spurs' faltering form and Cup disappointments, he had emerged from the recent months with credit and many believed he was one of the players who could force his way into the reckoning even at this late stage. It was a huge challenge but Eriksson's call-up for the Holland game in February suggested that the Tottenham man was very much in the manager's thoughts and still in contention.

The conventional wisdom – and Eriksson's previous selections – suggested that Rio Ferdinand, Sol Campbell and Middlesbrough's Gareth Southgate had already booked their place on the plane and, assuming the manager was planning to take four centre-backs, that meant there was one place for the taking.

Ledley, however, was not the only centre-half with World Cup aspirations. Middlesbrough's Ugo Ehiogu, Ledley's former Under-21 team-mate Jamie Carragher at Liverpool, Arsenal's Martin Keown and Leeds youngster Jonathan Woodgate were all pressing their own claims for inclusion and opinion in the media was split over whom Eriksson would finally pick.

It was certain, though, that Ledley could forget about spending his summer in Japan and South Korea if he didn't make the squad for the Italy game. Eriksson had made no secret of the fact he was now in the final stages his World Cup selection and preparation and any player not involved at Elland Road could safely book their summer holidays.

When the news came that Ledley was in the squad, the relief was mixed with a sense of anticipation. He was once again on the verge of winning his first England cap but he also knew his début, should it come against Italy, was now also effectively a World Cup trial. The stakes could not be any higher.

'Ledley was to have made his début against Holland, so it's important that he has another chance to show us what he can do,' Eriksson explained after unveiling his squad. 'I am looking for us to compete with one of the favourites for the World Cup. I have not seen the Italian team but they are strong everywhere. At the back, Italy have always been very strong defensively and, if they play Totti, Montella and Vieri upfront, that is a big challenge for us.'

Naturally, Ledley refused to be fazed by his inclusion or Eriksson's admission that he expected a difficult 90 minutes for England's back four. The laid-back 21-year-old insisted that he was simply happy to have been given another chance after his previously curtailed involvement in the squad and, although privately he knew how much was riding on the match, he tried to keep a low profile in the days before the game. He said, 'I was disappointed not to be well for the last game but, fingers crossed, I might get an opportunity this time. It's an important game and I'd love to be involved.'

When Eriksson announced his starting XI to face the Azzurri, Ledley, though, was not in the team. The England manager opted for a back four of Danny Mills, Southgate, Campbell and Wayne Bridge, and Ledley had to be content with a place on the bench. There was no doubt Eriksson would deploy a raft of substitutes at some point during the game and the chances of Ledley getting on still looked good.

Over 36,000 England fans packed into Elland Road to watch the match on 27 February but had to endure a cagey first-half during which both defences were on top and goal-scoring opportunities at a premium.

England's best chance came from a dead ball. Italy's Alessandro Nesta was penalised for holding Emile Heskey's shirt and David Beckham stepped up to send in one of his trademark curling free-kicks. The delivery was superb and it was Campbell, Ledley's former team-mate, who got on the end of it only to see 'keeper Gianluigi Buffon tip his effort over the bar.

Half-time brought a wave of anticipation among the supporters. Everyone in the ground expected the coach to make changes during the break and they were not disappointed when England came out for the second-half. Eriksson had made a total of nine substitutions and Ledley was one of them. He could call himself a full international player at last.

It was an ironic twist of fate that he came on for Campbell, the man he replaced in the heart of the Spurs defence and in the affections of the White Hart Lane faithful. Campbell was a certainty for the World Cup squad but the sense that the substitution was a dress rehearsal for a future changing of the guard was inescapable. Once again, David Pleat's words – 'The king is dead… long live the king' – seemed eerily appropriate.

If the first half at Leeds had been bereft of goals, the second 45 minutes more than compensated and it was England who drew first blood 18 minutes after the restart when Joe Cole took full advantage of a moment of indecision from Nesta and darted forward towards the Italian goal. As the defence closed in on him, Cole slid the ball into Robbie Fowler, who beat Buffon with a low, hard drive. England were in the driving seat.

But if Cole was the architect of England's opening goal, he was also unwittingly at the heart of Italy's equaliser. The West Ham midfielder was caught in possession in his own half by Gianluca Zambrotta. The ball was spread to striker Vincenzo Montella, who found space despite the attentions of Ehiogu and unleashed a curling left-footed shot that gave David James in the England goal no chance. The Azzurri were back on terms.

Playing at the back, Ledley looked relaxed and assured

but also managed to get forward at times and had one long-range effort on target that forced a save from Buffon. After that, the match seemed destined to peter out in a draw but there was one last moment of drama in store for the crowd in the dying minutes.

Italy mounted one last attack and surged into the England box. James came rushing out to dive at the feet of striker Massimo Maccarone but mistimed the challenge and, despite England's protests, the referee pointed to the spot. Montella was the man who stepped forward and coolly converted for his second of the match. The Azzurri had won with the last kick of the match and Ledley's long-awaited début had ended in defeat.

The result was only the second defeat of Eriksson's reign following his appointment 14 months earlier. It was not a devastating result in terms of England's World Cup preparations and the Swedish coach was eager to emphasis the positives in his post-match press conference. 'It disturbs me that we lost today but I am not worried,' Eriksson told the assembled media. 'The spirit is good. We played as good as Italy and they are more experienced. It's better to lose a friendly than a competitive game. We played equally well as Italy and they are one of the favourites for the World Cup. We were unlucky to lose the game. We lost it because of a lack of experience but, to gain experience, you have to play and make mistakes. It is important to see the individual players when you have to choose a 23-man squad. We missed a lot of players tonight but it was good for the youngsters.'

As one of those youngsters, Ledley had certainly done

his World Cup chances no harm at all. He had not made an unequivocal case for inclusion but he had slotted seamlessly into the side, defended neatly and used possession well. It was an assured if not spectacular début. 'I enjoyed it,' he said on his return to Spurs and the remainder of the domestic campaign. 'It was nice after missing the first match [against Holland] to finally get out there and it was thoroughly enjoyable. I think it was another step up and there's been a few this season that I have to keep adapting to. I think that was the biggest step so far. The concentration levels are that much higher, along with the sharpness and movement of players. It was definitely noticeable, the class of the Italian players, I could really tell out there.'

He added that he was pleased to have had a chance on goal as well, and thought that he'd taken his chance as well as he could have done. The 'keeper, though, had been top class, and made the save look easy. As for the future, Ledley made no secret of the fact that he had loved playing in an England shirt, and relished the chance to repeat the experience. He'd done his bit – now it was down to Sven-Göran Eriksson.

Life was certainly changing for Ledley. He was now an established Premiership player and, although hardly a household name at this stage, it wasn't just Spurs fans who were sitting up and taking notice of his talents. There was a growing consensus in the football fraternity that Tottenham had unearthed a genuine star and, still aged just 21, his best years were ahead of him.

The increasing public attention was not something he

was inherently comfortable with. After three seasons in the White Hart Lane first team, he understood that the media attention, as well as public adoration, came with the job but it was not a situation that he welcomed. Essentially a private man, Ledley would happily have disappeared off the face of the earth after an appearance for club or country, only to resurface for the next fixture. He was not an individual who was going to be changed one iota by his new-found fame.

'I just don't think of myself as famous,' he said in an interview when asked whether he was enjoying his celebrity status in the wake of becoming an England player. 'I've got so much more to do in the game to think that way. I'm still not recognised that much and I don't get asked to sign autographs. If I wasn't playing for Spurs on Sunday, I would probably go to watch my brother playing for my old club. It's time I did that because I haven't been to his matches that much lately and you should support your younger brother. Senrab have asked me in the past to present their club trophies and I've been very happy to do that – but I can't think of myself as some sort of celebrity.'

Celebrity or not, Ledley had to come back down to earth quickly after his England début as Spurs prepared for their game with Middlesbrough at the Riverside just three days later. The home side still had lingering relegation worries, while Tottenham's challenge was to ensure that a season of highs and lows did not limp inauspiciously towards the finishing line. Injuries dictated that Ledley was pressed into emergency service as right-back as Spurs looked for their second successive away win in the league.

The game was a free-flowing, entertaining affair from the first whistle and there were regular chances at both ends. The visitors just had the edge in the early exchanges and took a deserved lead on 32 minutes when Matthew Etherington delivered an inviting cross from the left which caught the Middlesbrough defence by surprise and Norwegian striker Steffen Iversen gratefully slammed home the opener.

The slender advantage lasted until the 69th minute when Anthony Gardener was adjudged to have pushed striker Alen Boksic, and Franck Queudrue stepped up to blast the resulting free-kick with a shot that almost burst the net. Substitute Teddy Sheringham could have stolen the points in the final minute of the match but his effort went inches wide and the spoils were shared.

A minor ankle injury forced Ledley to sit out the next game – a 2–1 victory over Leeds United at White Hart Lane – and, with the north London derby against Arsenal fast approaching, there was concern that the Spurs talisman could be unavailable. The Gunners were chasing the title and Tottenham could ill afford to be without their most reliable defender for the clash at Highbury.

The week before the big game, the signs were that he was winning his fitness race and the man himself was optimistic about his chances of making the starting line-up as he looked ahead to another clash with the club's oldest and fiercest rivals. 'I picked up a little knock on Saturday against Middlesbrough,' he told the Spurs website. 'It's nothing serious, just a little swelling around the ankle and shouldn't be a problem. I was jogging today [Wednesday] and it was just nice to be back out there having a little run and I'll see how it is. At the moment, I think it should be all right, it's still not 100 per cent but it might be well enough to get back in the squad.

'We've had three good results recently and we've got our confidence back. We're looking forward to the Arsenal game. We played them earlier in the season and I thought we deserved to win. It's going to be a tough game, we know that, but it's a derby game and the form book goes out of the window.

'They've got three or four top-quality strikers who are all different, all hard to play against, so you know you are in for a rough ride as a defender. This is the Premiership, though, and you're playing against tough players every week and you get used to it. They are great on the break and soak up the pressure. One long ball and they're off and they can score from things like that. That's one thing they can do really well – we know it's going to be a tough game.'

As befitting a young athlete of his stature, Ledley was eventually declared fit for the derby and the stage was set for another frenetic clash in north London. In fact, the stakes had been raised even further than usual earlier in the day when Manchester United beat Leicester City to throw down the gauntlet to Arsenal in their two-horse title race and, when the two sides ran out on to the Highbury pitch, the noise was deafening.

The early exchanges were predictably abrasive as the tackles flew in from every quarter and it was not until midway through the first half that the crowd witnessed a real moment of quality. Unfortunately, it was from Arsenal, as Dennis Bergkamp threaded a pass through to midfielder Freddie Ljungberg, who delicately chipped Kasey Keller to break the deadlock.

Spurs refused to buckle under the increasing pressure but their chances of keeping Arsenal at bay were dealt a serious blow as the half-time whistle loomed. Until then, Ledley had looked untroubled by his recent Achilles problems but he began limping slightly as the break approached. He refused to come off but it was obvious he was starting to struggle. Half-time came and went but, when Spurs emerged to resume hostilities, Ledley remained in the dressing room.

Without him, Tottenham acquitted themselves admirably, even though it required a dubious penalty award on 81 minutes for the side to draw level, courtesy of Sheringham's spot-kick. It seemed they would come away from Highbury with a draw but another penalty award just five minutes later – this time for the home side – put paid to that as Lauren fired home the winner.

The initial diagnosis on Ledley's injury was encouraging. It seemed the big defender had done nothing more serious than aggravate the Achilles rather than suffer a new setback and, despite his disappointment at missing the second half at Highbury and Spurs' narrow defeat, there was significant consolation just around the corner.

The day after the Arsenal match, the Professional Footballers' Association announced its annual nominations for Player and Young Player of the Year and, unsurprisingly,

Ledley's name was among the six in the Young Player category. Voted for by fellow professionals, the nomination was a fitting tribute to his outstanding performances over the course of what was his first full Premiership season and recognition of his growing maturity. The other nominees were Liverpool's Steven Gerrard, Newcastle striker Craig Bellamy, Aston Villa forward Darius Vassell, Michael Ricketts of Bolton and Ledley's former Under-21 team-mate John Terry of Chelsea.

Spurs skipper Teddy Sheringham was in no doubt that his young team-mate had earned his latest seal of approval from the wider football fraternity. 'He's definitely worthy of being in there,' Sheringham said. 'He's a 21-year-old, it's his first full season in the Premiership and he's been outstanding. He's probably been our most consistent player throughout the season and thoroughly deserves to be in there. If there was a little more recognition, he could well have got into the Player of the Year category. I'm sure he'll take this for the time being, though, and he's in there with a great calibre of players. He's a great lad, a team player and, when you play like that, your own performance always comes out on top and he fully deserves the credit he's getting. I think he has every chance of winning and I think he should win it.'

A week later the respective winners of the PFA gongs were announced and it was Bellamy rather than Ledley who scooped the young player award. It was a disappointment but his stubborn Achilles problem was more of a concern and he was forced to sit out Spurs' next Premiership fixture – a 1–1 stalemate with West Ham at

White Hart Lane. It was now touch and go whether he would be ready in time for the trip to Bolton.

'It doesn't feel too bad at the moment,' he said in the days leading up to the Reebok clash. 'I think I'll put it to the test this week and see how it responds. It was a kick initially, but there might have been a problem in there before that which has probably come up. It's a bit of a shame because I've only missed a few games but it's still been a good season for me overall.'

Unfortunately, his optimism proved to be misguided and he stayed in north London as the rest of the squad headed north for the Bolton game. Spurs had just two league games left to play – at home to Liverpool and away at Leicester – and it now seemed Ledley's injury was going to bring an end to his season prematurely. After staying injury-free for the majority of the season, it was a bitter pill to swallow.

Worse still, his involvement with England in the summer was also under real threat. His place in Eriksson's senior squad was far from guaranteed but, if he did fail to make the World Cup cut, it was an absolute certainty that David Platt would turn the omission to his advantage and include the Spurs man in his Under-21 party for the European Championships in Switzerland.

The football world waited with bated breath when, in early May, Eriksson finally announced the 23 players going to the World Cup. It was the day before the final round of Premiership games of the season and it was time for all the speculation, rumours and debate to end.

The news for Ledley was not good. Eriksson had

decided to dispense with his services in favour of a centre-half quartet of Campbell, Ferdinand, Southgate and Keown and he wouldn't be going to Japan and South Korea. His late surge into the England reckoning had got him close but, in the end, it was not enough to dislodge older, more experienced players.

Eriksson was reluctant to talk publicly about the players he had to leave behind but there was no doubt Ledley's inactivity for a month had not helped his cause. The big defender had been denied the opportunity to further his claims just as the England coach was finalising his squad and it would have been a huge gamble to include him in the final 23 when there were still concerns about his fitness. It was heartache for Ledley but, from Eriksson's perspective, it was the only decision he could make.

David Platt, however, had no such reservations and, as soon as it was confirmed that Ledley had not made the cut, he named him in the Under-21 squad destined for Switzerland. The World Cup's loss would be England's gain at the European Under-21 Championships. Platt was brimming with confidence ahead of the competition and being able to call Ledley back into the heart of his defence was an unexpected bonus.

'With the players we have available, I believe we can win the tournament,' he told the FA website. 'From the day I took the job, I believed we could get through because of the names that we have at our disposal. There is huge talent there and I have to trust it. The squad is a team of winners and you only need to look at the level of football that they are playing to see that they stand an excellent chance of going to Euro 2004. Some of them are playing in the Champions League and more than a few of them are playing regularly in big Premiership games. When you think about the stage they are at in their careers and then think about how young they are, it is startling.'

The Achilles injury cleared up sufficiently for Ledley to report for Under-21 duty. He was still coming to terms with Eriksson's snub but he was also philosophical and desperate to make an impression in Switzerland. The only question was whether his ankle would allow him to play a full part in the tournament. 'It is still a bit sore at the moment,' he admitted. 'It definitely has got better but I can still feel it. I'm not really sure what's going to happen from here yet. The Under-21s is a bit of a problem at the moment to be honest. We'll see how it goes.'

His anxiety sadly proved to be justified and, just two days after joining up with his Under-21 team-mates, he was on a plane back to London. The Achilles stubbornly refused to heal and, rather than risk aggravating the problem, the England management team decided to send him home to rest and recuperate. Ledley's summer plans lay in tatters. It was a cruel end to what had been a hugely successful season for the 21-year-old. He had been a virtual ever-present in the Tottenham line-up prior to his injury at Middlesbrough in late March, earned his first England cap and had been recognised by his peers at the PFA. He had also established himself as one of the first names on Glenn Hoddle's team sheet and he was already acknowledged as one of the Premiership's most naturally-gifted young defenders.

A summer of rehabilitation had not been part of the plan and Ledley, like millions of expectant England fans, was forced to watch events unfold at the World Cup on the television. England eventually progressed through to the last eight of the tournament to face Brazil and, despite his personal disappointment, the Spurs man was glued to the action like everyone else. 'I would love to be out there, definitely, there's a bit of envy,' he told the Spurs website. 'It's where any player would want to be. A quarter-final of the World Cup against Brazil – it would be the pinnacle of your career. England are doing superbly at the moment, fantastic. We've played really well and defended as well as anyone and Rio Ferdinand has been outstanding. I think Brazil will be a tight game and England can win it, 1–0 perhaps.' His confidence in the side, however, proved misplaced and, despite taking the lead through Michael Owen in the first-half, England were beaten 2–1 and heading home.

The summer at White Hart Lane saw Glenn Hoddle conduct a systematic clear-out of the older players in the first team. Tim Sherwood, Chris Armstrong and Oyvind Leonhardsen were all allowed to leave as the manager strived to instil a more youthful feel to his squad, and the fans waited in anticipation to see which players Hoddle would recruit to fill the gaps.

The big money went on strikers. Republic of Ireland front-man Robbie Keane was signed from cash-strapped Leeds United in a £7 million deal, while Hoddle cast his net further afield for another option, landing Portuguese forward Helder Postiga from Porto for £6.25 million.

What was significant was that the Tottenham boss did not feel the need to bolster his defence. The finances were in place to bring in new faces but Hoddle evidently had ample faith in Ledley and his fellow defenders. It was exactly the statement of intent the injured star need as he battled to regain full fitness.

The club's annual pre-season trip to La Manga in Spain presented the defender with a chance to continue his recovery in warmer climes and, as Spurs prepared for high-profile friendlies against Celtic and Italian giants Lazio in early August 2002, the indications were he was winning his battle to regain full fitness. He made it clear that everything was progressing well, and that he'd been training fully with the rest of the squad. The rest at the end of the summer seemed to have done him a power of good, and he hoped to participate fully in the upcoming friendlies against Celtic and Lazio. If Tottenham were going to press for serious European contention, then they had to test themselves against decent European opposition – with players like Henrik Larsson and Chris Sutton for Celtic, and World Cup stars such as Crespo, Simeone, Nesta and Mendieta for Lazio – and the friendlies presented a great opportunity to do just that.

'Both matches should be very entertaining for the fans,' Ledley said. 'These are the kind of games they want to be watching at White Hart Lane and I'm sure they will be great for them to watch and great for the players to be involved in.'

Ledley, however, was to play no part in either game as what now seemed to be an injury jinx cruelly struck again as he damaged his hip while jogging on the Spurs training ground. It was an innocuous way to get injured but it would set back his recovery and return to the first team for another three months. He may have been an athletic, naturally-gifted player with the best years of his career firmly ahead of him, but he certainly wasn't the luckiest footballer.

'Ledley hasn't really done anything in pre-season,' Hoddle admitted in August. 'He's done this week's training but still feels a little discomfort. Unfortunately, he's had a little jolt backwards, nothing major. He's been training fine but overnight it had stiffened up, so we have to be a bit careful on that one. We've got to rest him for a few more days. It's a blow for us. He needs to overcome the injury and then get himself fit.'

Tottenham were forced to begin the new campaign without their talismanic defender and, initially, they prospered in the Premiership even without him. An opening day draw with Everton at Goodison was followed by three successive wins over Aston Villa, Charlton and Southampton and, although a last-minute defeat at Craven Cottage against Fulham in a 3–2 thriller brought Spurs back down to earth with a bump, the signs were that Ledley would return to a side in rude health when his hip problem was finally sorted out.

The burning question was when exactly that would be. His 22nd birthday in October came and went and still he had not tasted any competitive action. The wait for Ledley, his manager, his team-mates and the Tottenham supporters was proving longer than anyone had imagined.

It was to be November until there was good news.

Midway through the month, he came through a reserve team game against Leicester City unscathed – his second appearance for the second-string side – and played the full 90 minutes. He was now close to making it back into the first team. They certainly needed him back in the trenches as soon as possible. A shock third-round League Cup defeat at the hands of Burnley had severely dented the team's confidence and that had been followed by a 2–0 defeat at Sunderland in the league. Spurs were in real danger of throwing away what had been an encouraging start to the 2002/03 campaign.

Ledley's scheduled comeback game could not have presented a more dramatic prospect for the young defender – the north London derby at Highbury. It was far from an ideal, 'ease-yourself-back-into-the-Premiership -gently' fixture. As always, it would be a game in which no quarter would be given or asked for and Hoddle was faced with a dilemma. Should he risk Ledley in the Highbury cauldron or should he wrap him in cotton wool and wait for a more a less potentially explosive affair?

In the end, Hoddle decided to be bold and named Ledley in his starting XI. His last appearance had been 45 minutes against the Gunners at the Lane back in April and now, more than six months later, he was to return to the ranks against the same side.

The match was not short of controversy but, thankfully, none of it was connected with Ledley's fitness. Arsenal were quicker out of the blocks in the first half on their own patch and took the lead after 13 minutes when Thierry Henry finished off a counter-attack with a neat placement past Kasey Keller. Tottenham were already facing an uphill struggle at a ground where they had not tasted victory since 1993, and the task became almost impossible a little later in the half when they found themselves reduced to ten men.

The player heading for the early bath was Welsh international Simon Davies, who found himself on the wrong end of two dubious decisions by referee Mike Riley. Riley booked Davies in the 22nd minute for a tackle on Ashley Cole. Four minutes later he showed Davies a second yellow for an innocuous challenge on Patrick Vieira. Davies had to go.

Spurs held out until the break, but the second-half saw Arsenal increase the pressure and it was inevitable that further goals would come. Freddie Ljungberg added the second on 55 minutes and Sylvain Wiltord completed the scoring with nineteen minutes to go. Tottenham had to leave Highbury empty-handed again.

But there was further controversy before the final whistle when Ledley landed awkwardly on Ljungberg's knee and the Swedish midfielder was forced off. The Arsenal players were unhappy with the challenge and, although Riley took no action, after the match Ledley was accused of stamping on the Swede. The Football Association quickly confirmed it had requested a video of the incident and it suddenly seemed his long-awaited comeback was to about to ruined by disciplinary proceedings. For his part, Ledley was adamant there had been no malice in his contact with the Arsenal man. 'I did tread on him but it was not deliberate in any way,' he insisted after the game. 'It was a complete accident and I could do nothing else because of my momentum. I could not get out of the way and, if you look at my disciplinary record, you will see I am not a dirty player. I would never stamp on anyone.'

It had been a miserable 90 minutes in all for Hoddle, who was particularly aggrieved at Davies' red card and the accusation that Ledley had deliberately set out to injure an opponent. 'We're very disappointed,' he said. 'I think the referee has to have a look at it and change his view on it. Simon hasn't made any contact at all and I'm not saying Ashley [Cole] did anything wrong, I've watched it back myself, but certainly on video it shows that no contact was made and it has cost us.' As far as the accusations over the 'deliberate' stamp on Ljungberg went, Hoddle reiterated that he saw nothing deliberate in Ledley's actions, and pointed out that Ljungberg hadn't accused Ledley of anything at all. He, too, felt that the players momentum had made contact inevitable, and unavoidable.

It was had not been the kind of comeback Ledley had envisaged during his long months of rehabilitation but, the day after the Arsenal game, he received news that would quickly help erase the painful memories of the Highbury mauling.

England were to get together later in the month for a two-day training camp – as well as visit Buckingham Palace for an audience with the Queen – and despite having played one match in six months, Sven-Göran Eriksson asked Ledley to join up with the rest of the squad. The England boss may have overlooked him for the summer's World Cup finals, but the latest invitation was clear evidence that Ledley was still very much in his thoughts. He was only just back in the Spurs team but his England career seemed destined for a kick-start.

There was further positive news when the FA decided that Ledley had no case to answer following the Ljungberg incident and he was free to concentrate on building up his match sharpness. There was a lot of missed time to make up for.

The news of the call-up was also warmly welcomed back at White Hart Lane. The club's coaching staff had witnessed at close quarters the difficult battle to overcome his injury problems and coach Chris Hughton was convinced that Ledley would enjoy a bright international future. 'I can remember him playing in the youth team and Ledley was one that, if you were watching, he would stand out,' he told the Spurs website. 'Sometimes he would do two or three things at the back, show real composure, bring the ball down instead of panicking and kicking it away. He would have more composure than others.

'It is a wonderful bonus for us that he has come through the youth system here. The thing is, he's still just at the start of his career. The position he plays is a mature position. Generally, the best centre-halves don't reach their peaks until they are 28 or 29 years of age when they can combine the qualities they've got with that maturity and leadership you need in that position. He's got it all in front of him as a future international, most definitely.

'His priority at the moment has to be to get himself fit and to play games here but certainly he has a wonderfully bright future. He has a big frame but he's comfortable enough on the ball to cope with the pressures and pace of the modern game and the abilities of the players he's playing.

'If you look at international defenders, the vast majority will not only be able to defend but also distribute the ball. They have that composure, particularly at international level where the game is faster and more frantic than in the Premiership and most national leagues. As an international player, he is someone you would think has a future.'

Back in the Premiership, Spurs were to play host to Leeds United and were desperate to get back to winning ways. It was only Ledley's second start of the season but he was already close to his majestic best at the Lane as Tottenham coasted to a comfortable 2–0 win courtesy of goals from Teddy Sheringham and Robbie Keane. It was a result that took them up to seventh in the table and seemed to represent a turning of the corner for both the team and Ledley himself.

'We've been on an indifferent run and, although we've been playing well at the Lane, we haven't been here for a while,' Hoddle said in his press conference after the game. 'It is good to come back and put on a good performance and get three points. We're delighted. We played well in the first half and might have come in with more than 2–0. As a coach, though, you are looking for your next win and we are delighted with the way we passed the ball. We got a clean sheet as well, so there is something to build on.

'This is a tight league now... we've got to make sure this is the beginning of a little run for us because things can happen. You look at the league and it is so close. Two wins turn it round for you; two losses and it can go the other way... it is as tight as that at the moment. There is a lot of football still to be played. I am delighted with the work rate and the way that we played. We've won the game and we deserved to.'

A hard-earned draw at St Andrews against Birmingham and a 3–1 home victory over West Brom continued the momentum as the team headed into the hectic Christmas period but, before the flurry of festive fixtures, there was the return match with Arsenal at the Lane.

Exactly how the Premiership fixture computer threw up the second north London derby of the season exactly a month after the first was a mystery, but it gave Spurs an early opportunity to avenge their defeat at Highbury. And this time, Ledley was fully fit and, with four successful comeback games under his belt, there was no question of him not being able to adapt to the pace of what was sure to be another adrenalin-fuelled clash.

It is difficult to overstate the importance of his return to Spurs colours. Although not a natural communicator on the pitch, his cool approach to the game invariably had a calming effect on those around him and this quiet influence wasn't lost on his team-mates. 'To look like he's playing under as little pressure as he does is very comforting,' admitted Spurs' keeper Kasey Keller when asked what Ledley's main strength was. 'He's a very talented young man and, if he stays fit and focused, there is no reason why he can't be one of the top defenders in the league for many, many years to come.'

White Hart Lane was packed to the rafters for the

132nd instalment of one of the footballs' most famous grudge matches and, from the start, Spurs played with a sense of purpose and control that made a mockery of their recent performance across the other side of north London. They applied all the early pressure and it came as no surprise that they took the lead on eleven minutes. Gus Poyet was hauled down by Ray Parlour 30 yards from goal, and Christian Ziege stepped up to blast the resulting free-kick past David Seaman in the Arsenal goal. The advantage was almost doubled just three minutes later when Dean Richards out-jumped the defence only to see his header cleared off the line by Ashley Cole. And it was Cole again who got the visitors out of jail midway through the half, this time clearing Robbie Keane's shot off the line with Seaman beaten.

Spurs were in the ascendancy but, in the final minute of the first half, Keller was to have an inexplicable rush of blood that led to Arsenal's equaliser. The visitors pumped a long, hopeful ball forward for Thierry Henry to chase and, although there appeared to be no immediate danger, Keller came charging out and clipped the striker's heels just inside the box. Referee Neale Barry had no choice but to point to the spot and Robert Pires duly stepped up to convert the penalty.

The second-half failed to produce the fireworks of the first and, although Keane had two presentable chances, there was no further score. On the evidence of the first 45 minutes, Hoddle's side were worthy of all three points but, after their chastening experience at Highbury four weeks earlier, no one was complaining about a share of the spoils and an infinitely more commanding and entertaining performance.

'We're definitely happy with the way we performed, but a little bit disappointed that we didn't manage to get the three points,' Ledley admitted. 'I'd say it was definitely one of our best performances of the season… It's nice to play that way and we just want to see if we can continue like that and take it to other teams where I'm sure we will get the three points.'

The prediction would be put to the test in the next match against Manchester City at Maine Road. Just two days before Christmas, a victory or a draw would extend Spurs' unbeaten run to five and, having won at the same ground the previous season, confidence was high.

City, however, applied all the early pressure and took the lead on the half-hour when centre-half Steve Howey headed home, but the score seemed to jolt the visitors into life and, ten minutes later, Chris Perry levelled with his first of the season.

Shortly after the break, Simon Davies got the goal his impressive all-round performance deserved and Gus Poyet made it 1–3 late on. The match seemed done and dusted, although Christian Ziege's subsequent sending-off and a second City goal from Ali Benarbia ensured some nervous final moments before the final whistle.

Boxing Day produced a 2–2 draw with Charlton at the Lane in the London derby but the wheels then began to fall off the Spurs bandwagon. A narrow 2–1 defeat at Newcastle was followed by defeat by a single goal at Southampton, Hoddle's old club, when James Beattie stole a march on former team-mate Dean Richards and snatched a late winner. It was not a crisis but, after an encouraging run, it was a setback.

Perhaps the New Year would usher in a change of fortune. The Premiership was put on hold to make way for the third round of the FA Cup and, as fate would have it, Tottenham were drawn against the Saints at St Mary's. It was only three days after the two sides' league meeting and Hoddle and his charges were determined to avoid a repeat performance.

The first game had been played in atrocious conditions and, although Tottenham's display should have earned them a point on the south coast, Ledley was clear the Spurs defence needed to shackle Beattie more effectively in the Cup clash if they were to progress.

'He is a handful and has scored a lot of goals this season,' he told the club website. 'I thought we handled him quite well, but it just goes to show because he popped up at the end there and won it for them.'

Tottenham's cause was not helped by the loss of Richards with an Achilles injury. Ledley's pre-match warning about Beattie seemed to go unheeded as the burly striker almost single-handedly put Spurs out of the cup. First, Kasey Keller failed to hold on to his well-driven free-kick and Michael Svensson gratefully gobbled up the scraps. After the break, it was Beattie who set up Jo Tessem for Southampton's second and, although he played no part in the third from Anders Svensson, it was no surprise that he grabbed the fourth for himself with a close-range effort. Spurs had been badly mauled.

Hoddle was in no mood to try and put a positive spin on events after the game and it was obvious he felt the result represented one of the lowest moments of his 20-month tenure as manager. 'We deserved more in the league game last week but, playing like that today, we deserved what we got,' the manager conceded. He admitted that Southampton deserved credit for the way they had played, but he was extremely disappointed at the work rate and quality on the ball of his team. He also felt that they had all let the fans down, and that could not be allowed to happen in the next home match against Everton. He concluded by saying, 'I am feeling sick at the moment because I know we can do better.'

But it was not all doom and gloom. Although they were in ninth in the table after failing to pick up any points in their last two games, they were only three points off the top six places and another good run of results could see the team force their way into the European places. Victory over Everton, who were also in the hunt for a UEFA Cup place, would be a huge step in the right direction.

With so much at stake, the match could have been a cautious, cagey affair with both sides unwilling to chance their arm at White Hart Lane but, whether by design or default, the two teams conspired to produce arguably the most dramatic clash of the Premiership season.

The match began at a dizzying pace and it was Everton who made the initial breakthrough after just ten minutes. Toffees midfielder Scott Gemmill pounced on a loose ball and threaded an inch-perfect pass through to American débutante Brian McBride, who had only signed for the club on loan from Columbus Crew earlier in the week. The striker showed no signs of jet-lag however as he calmly slotted the ball past compatriot Kasey Keller.

The lead lasted a mere three minutes. Spurs won a corner, Simon Davies nodded on to Poyet and the veteran Uruguayan planted a firm header past former Tottenham 'keeper Espen Baardsen. There were more chances for both sides before the break but they went in all square at half-time, evidently saving the lion's share of the fireworks for the second 45 minutes.

The match exploded into life just five minutes after the restart when Robbie Keane beat the offside trap and latched on to Darren Anderton's long pass, rounded Baardsen and rolled the ball into the empty net. Everton were back on terms soon after when Steve Watson was allowed to steal into the area unmarked and score from close range and, with less than an hour on the clock, the match had already produced four goals.

Tottenham got their noses back in front with Keane's second. This time, it was a delicious solo effort as he evaded a lunge by Joseph Yobo, turned on a sixpence and unleashed a 20-yard shot that beat Baardsen in the bottom-left corner. Spurs were back in the driving seat.

Under manager David Moyes, however, Everton were nothing if not tenacious and incredibly they equalised for a second time in the match when Polish striker Tomasz Radzinski found space ten yards out and beat Keller with a well-placed shot. The two teams were locked at 3–3 but few in the crowd believed that the game had seen its last goal. They were right. Roared on by the partisan crowd,

Spurs continued to push forward for the winner and, yet again, it was Keane who supplied the finish. A mistake by Alan Stubbs gifted the Republic of Ireland striker possession in the Everton half and, once he had evaded Yobo for a second crucial time, he bore down on goal and chipped Baardsen for his hat-trick and the winning goal. At last, Spurs had won a roller-coaster of a game 4–3.

Ledley and the rest of the Spurs defence were not happy with the three goals Everton scored but Hoddle understandably wanted to accentuate the positives at the other end of the match once he, his players and the fans had finally caught their breath.

'It was hard work, but we're absolutely delighted to take the three points,' he beamed. 'We had to churn it out in the end. We showed magnificent character. The most valuable thing for us this week was three points and I was very pleased with the manner we did it in the second half – great character, great play and what a magnificent hat-trick from Robbie Keane.'

Although football is a team game, different players take to the pitch with different priorities and ambitions. A striker lives to see the ball rippling the back of the net while a defender's innately miserly nature dictates they're never happier then when their goalkeeper is bored to tears. Hoddle may have been content to overlook Everton's three successful forays into the Spurs box, but Ledley could not. Although the side had ended their three-game losing sequence, they hadn't kept a clean sheet in the league since the victory over Leeds United at the Lane in November and it was becoming a bone of contention for the England man.

A week later, Spurs ventured to the Midlands to face Aston Villa at Villa Park. Hoddle was able to recall Dean Richards to partner Ledley in the middle of the defence after a two-week injury lay-off and, from the first whistle, the pair gave the side the defensive solidity they had been missing. Villa never looked like scoring.

Tottenham themselves were nowhere near as potent going forward as they had been against Everton, but a moment of pure quality from Teddy Sheringham was enough to separate the two sides, the veteran striker volleying home Stephen Carr's cross after 69 minutes. It was the only goal of the match and Spurs had their first win at Villa Park for 17 years.

Richards was voted Man of the Match after a commanding display alongside Ledley, who had finally got the clean sheet he cherished and, after the game, he was more than happy to pay tribute to his centre-half partner. 'Dean dominates the forwards and it gives you confidence playing alongside him,' he said. 'I think our last clean sheet was against Leeds – quite a while back – so we wanted another one. We mainly wanted the three points, but a clean sheet is an added bonus. It's such a tough league with a lot of teams fighting it out. If we can put a little run together, I'm sure we can shoot right up there. That is our aim.'

To put together this run, Spurs needed to see off the challenge of Newcastle and, for 89 minutes at White Hart Lane, it at least seemed the home side would earn a share of the points as both teams fired blanks in front of goal.

The old adage that you've got to play for the full 90

minutes was never more apt, however, as Spurs fatally gave Craig Bellamy too much space and, although Keller managed to keep his shot out, Jermaine Jenas was on hand to scramble home the loose ball. There were just 25 seconds left of normal time and Tottenham had been caught by a classic sucker punch. Ledley had also been robbed of a second successive clean sheet.

There were only three days in which to dissect what had gone wrong. Spurs were due to make the journey across London to Stamford Bridge and, for Ledley, it would be a chance to cross swords with a familiar face from his past. By now, his old Senrab team-mate John Terry had established himself in the Blues first team and, like Ledley, he was earning widespread praise for his all-action performances. Unlike Ledley, he was yet to play for the England senior team, despite having excelled for the Under-21s, but together they were regarded as the natural successors to Sol Campbell and Rio Ferdinand in the heart of the England defence.

'John's a good player,' Ledley told the Spurs website as he looked ahead to the showdown at Stamford Bridge. 'He used to play in midfield when we were younger and you could see his qualities then. So I am not surprised he's done so well. He had a growth spurt and shot up, but even when he was quite short, he was good in the air. Because of that, I am not surprised he has dropped to the back.

'Chelsea are playing well at the moment and we know it's going to be a tough game. We normally bounce back quickly from a defeat so that is what we are looking to do again. We still take a bit of confidence from how we beat them 5–1 last season. We know that we can beat them and that is the approach we've got to take.'

The opening salvos in west London certainly seemed to suggest that Ledley's upbeat assessment was well founded. Spurs looked and played like the home side and both Sheringham and Simon Davies should have done better with good early chances but their profligacy in front of goal was soon forgotten after eighteen minutes when Sheringham slid in to poke home Darren Anderton's cross. The visitors had got their noses in front and were beginning to dream of the club's first win at Stamford Bridge since 1986.

The dream nearly turned into a nightmare on the half-hour when a scramble in the Spurs area looked destined to result in a goal. Tottenham seemed incapable of clearing the ball and, when Gianfranco Zola got an inadvertent touch, it looked as though Chelsea simply had to equalise, only for Ledley to make a dramatic goal-line clearance.

The tension was increasing by the minute and referee Paul Durkin had to intervene to prevent the game boiling over towards the end of the half when opposing full-backs Stephen Carr and Graeme Le Saux were involved in a fracas. Carr had put the ball into touch to allow Anthony Gardener to get treatment, but Le Saux took a quick throw-in and the pair had a heated face-to-face exchange before Durkin managed to calm them down. The atmosphere was even getting to the respective benches as Spurs assistant manager John Gorman and Chelsea boss Claudio Ranieri were pacified by fourth official Graham Poll.

Chelsea were back on terms five minutes before the

break. Ledley had manfully denied Zola earlier in the match but the big centre was powerless to stop the little Italian this time. Blues midfielder Boudewijn Zenden hit the turf outside the Spurs penalty area to earn his side a free-kick and Zola stepped up to deliver a curling shot that arced into the top right-hand corner of the net.

The second half saw Kasey Keller make a string of saves to keep Tottenham in the hunt and substitute Matthew Etherington could have stolen the points late on but shot straight at Carlo Cudicini, so the London rivals had to content themselves with a draw. It had been a full-blooded game and it would have been harsh for either side to have lost.

Ledley's commanding display could not have been better timed. Four days later, Sven-Göran Eriksson was due to announce his England squad for the friendly against Australia the following week and Ledley's typically calm performance in the fiery Stamford Bridge clash was a purposeful reminder of his international credentials. He was still only 14 games into his comeback after the hip injury but he was now back to his muscular, athletic best. A second England cap now looked a real possibility and his early season woes were now an increasingly distant memory.

Eriksson would wait until after Saturday's round of Premiership games before unveiling the squad to avoid including injured players, so it was vital that Ledley negotiated Spurs' match with Sunderland at White Hart Lane without incident. Thankfully, it was to be a gentle procession against the toothless Black Cats.

edley King lived and breathed football from an early age. He quickly graduated from
e concrete pitch near his childhood home to training with Leyton Orient and on to
ottenham Hotspur – who since 1995 have helped make him the accomplished defender
feared by Premiership rivals.

© *PA Photos*

Above left: Ledley has dedicated years of his life to working hard at the training ground, both for Spurs and England. He says that a full pre-season training programme gets him in shape and boosts his confidence.
© PA Photo

Above right: Despite spending agonising months out of action, Ledley closely followed his team's progress in the Premiership, including this fixture away to Portsmouth in August 2005.
© Sportsbe

Bottom left: At the January 2006 match against Aston Villa, Ledley proudly wore a shirt emblazoned with the new Spurs emblem.
© Sportsbe

Bottom right: In addition to the hours spent on the pitch and in the fitness centre, Ledle' doesn't hesitate to dedicate time to promote his club. This studio shot appeared on the Spurs website.
© Mirrorp

op: Facing the press in 2006.

© *PA Photos*

ottom left: In the thick of it at England's October 2005 World Cup Qualifier ;ainst Poland.

© *Sportsbeat*

ottom right: At a pre-season friendly against Stevenage Borough, tussling th Adam Miller.

© *Sportsbeat*

Top: Despite Ledley's best efforts, Spurs' impressive unbeaten run in the Premiership finally came to an end with a 3 – 1 defeat at Reading in November 2006. © *Clevamec*

Bottom left: Taking charge in a north London derby against Arsenal, April 2007.

© *Clevamec*

Bottom right: A crucial match against Man City in May 2007. © *Ge*

hough still affected by injury, under Ledley's captaincy, Spurs progressed well in the
)07 UEFA Cup. Their run came to an end at the quarter final stage against Sevilla.

op left: Running with the ball moments after he received a standing ovation from the
purs faithful.

© *Getty*

ottom left: Jermaine Jenas and Ledley react at the final whistle.

© *Clevamedia*

ottom right: Martin Jol hugs a dejected Ledley King and Tom Huddlestone at the end
f the match.

© *Clevamedia*

On international duty, October 2005.

© PA Photo

ttenham's 2006 UEFA Cup campaign showcased Ledley's string of impressive
rformances that had established him as one of the finest centre-halves in Europe.

p: With Jermaine Jenas against Club Brugge. © *Sportsbeat*

ttom: Away at Bayer Leverkusen, where Ledley's team-mate Berbatov scored against
former club. © *Sportsbeat*

Top: A moment of calm captures Ledley in a reflective mood while on international duty.

© PA Phot

Left: Taking a trip south of the river to the David Beckham Academy in Greenwich.

© REX Featur

Sunderland actually took a surprise lead in London through Kevin Phillips but it was one-way traffic after that. Gus Poyet scored his 50th league goal in England to get the ball rolling, Gary Doherty made it two and Simon Davies added the third. The stage was now set for Teddy Sheringham, who completed the scoring and, in the process, notched up the 300th goal of his club career.

Later the same day, Eriksson made his announcement and, as many had predicted, Ledley was back in the England fold. Although the likes of Manchester United's Gary Neville, David Beckham, Rio Ferdinand and Paul Scholes, as well as West Ham 'keeper David James, were experienced international performers, it was an experimental squad with a lot of young players like Ledley at the start of what they hoped would be long England careers. The youngest to be included was Everton's precocious 17-year-old striker Wayne Rooney and, unlike when he had made his début almost exactly a year ago against Italy, Ledley was far from the baby of the party this time around.

England had not lost to Australia in five previous meetings between the two countries but, with a raft of English-based players in Frank Farina's Socceroos squad, they had high expectations of springing a major surprise at Upton Park. England could certainly ill afford to take the game lightly.

Although he opted to give Southampton striker James Beattie his début in the starting XI, Eriksson otherwise named what was perceived as his strongest side for the start of the match. The pundits and supporters alike expected wholesale changes from the coach at half-time but, from the kick-off at least, Eriksson appeared to paying the Australians the compliment of sending out his crack troops.

What followed in the first 45 minutes was certainly not in the script. England looked nervous, disjointed and lacking in imagination against their less illustrious opponents. Australia sensed that an upset was on the cards and, after a mere seventeen minutes, the Socceroos pierced the English defence for the first time. The visitors won a free-kick near the box, Stan Lazaridis delivered an inviting cross into the danger area and Tony Popovic lost his marker Neville to head home past David James. It was woeful defending and Australia were in front.

If the England fans at Upton Park thought the goal would sting their side into life, they were to be sorely disappointed and, once again, England's much-vaunted defence was at fault. This time it was Ferdinand, four minutes before the break, who was the culprit when he was dispossessed by Harry Kewell. The winger took full advantage of Ferdinand's generosity, skipped past James and slid the ball into the back of the net. England were in disarray and Australia were two up.

Half-time came as a huge relief for Eriksson and his team and the coach began to make the raft of substitutions that everyone had anticipated. In fact, he sent out a completely different XI as Paul Robinson replaced James in goal, Danny Mills came on for Neville, Wes Brown replaced Ferdinand and, as had been the case 12 months earlier, Ledley came on for his old team-mate Campbell.

The Spurs defender instantly graduated from the ranks of the one-cap wonders and he had 45 minutes to make an impression. It was a difficult task with England below par and 11 new players trying to find their feet, but Ledley didn't care. He was back where he belonged and his immediate task was to shore up a defence that had looked alarmingly porous in the first half.

The change of personnel visibly gave England a lift after the break and Brown and Ledley ensured Australia's attacking threat was dulled as the match wore on. Robinson was untroubled in goal and England began pushing forward with renewed confidence. The goal had to come and it was Arsenal striker Francis Jeffers who supplied it, glancing home Jermaine Jenas' 69th-minute cross past Mark Schwarzer in the Australian goal. England's second string were making an infinitely better fist of the job than the more senior players and the crowd roared them on as they searched for the equaliser.

With the benefit of hindsight, England's enthusiastic youngsters pushed too hard and they were caught seven minutes from time with a classic counter-attack. Substitute striker John Aloisi fed Brett Emerton, who beat Robinson and the Socceroos had their famous victory.

The press licked their collective lips. A 3–1 defeat was the perfect stick with which to beat Eriksson. There was growing fan and media disquiet at his approach to friendlies and the wholesale substitutions he continued to make, disrupting the flow of the game and invariably ruining the entertainment value. The perceived débâcle against Australia was the perfect case in point and there was little sympathy for the England coach on the back pages the following morning. Under the headline 'KANGA POO', the *Sun* lambasted the 'total and utter shambles' of England's first-half performance, while the *Daily Mail* was no less scathing with their 'SHOCKEROOS' offering. 'We expected a farce,' wrote Jeff Powell in the paper, 'but it turned out to be a mockery.'

Eriksson, of course, was bullish about the team's second-half display. 'Nobody likes to lose a football game,' he argued. 'The boys did very well in the second half and you could see that there were a lot of talented players out there. I told them, "You have to go out and sort it out," and they almost did it. Some of the youngsters are almost ready for bigger tasks.'

From Ledley's perspective, the media backlash was a blow. The coach rather than the player himself was the target for widespread criticism but the result and the negative coverage of the game only served to detract from what, for Ledley, had been another 45 minutes in an England shirt. That Wayne Rooney had become the youngest ever England player at the age of 17 years and 111 days further shifted the agenda.

There were people in the know who acknowledged his display but their voices tended to be drowned out in the frenzied post-match outcry. 'When the dishevelled seniors departed at the break,' wrote Henry Winter in the *Daily Telegraph*, 'England looked far more secure defensively, where Ledley King and Wes Brown worked well in tandem, far more assertive in midfield, where Jenas and Owen Hargreaves excelled, and particularly, far more adventurous in attack, where Jeffers scored and Rooney threatened throughout.'

There was also praise from the Football Association's acting technical director Les Reed, who had helped oversee the development of Ledley and his contemporaries through the junior ranks all the way to the senior team. 'Obviously, to look on and see the line-up against Australia that Sven selected for the second-half tonight – with every single one of those players having come through our system – is tremendously satisfying,' Reed told the FA website. 'I know that I have personally coached all of them at some stage except [Owen] Hargreaves. Increasing the amount of progression that there is from Under-21 level to the senior side is one of the target ratios we set out to improve back in 1998. These days, we are able to school our players in international football right the way through the system and we are only just starting to see the real fruits of the work that we have put in over the last five years.'

Ledley himself was unperturbed by the furore in the wake of the headline-grabbing reverse. From his perspective, he had begun the season on the sidelines for club and country. His first senior appearance of the campaign only came in mid-November but, despite these obstacles, he had forced his way back into the England reckoning. He had been denied the opportunity to build on his impressive début against Italy the previous season and, at this stage of his career, he was simply happy to be back in England contention. That his 45 minutes of action, alongside a clutch of other young players, had seen a marked improvement in England's performance, was the icing on the cake.

'Once I got the call, I was just hoping nothing would go wrong,' Ledley admitted. 'It was nice to be out there again. We always knew we were going to play the second half and that gave us the chance to prepare. We didn't have anything to lose and went out and gave it our best shot. I thought we did OK. There are a lot of players and it will be hard for all of us to break into the squad but we were all glad to get that opportunity.'

Back in the Premiership, the battle for a UEFA Cup place was intensifying and the side knew victory over Fulham at White Hart Lane could propel them into sixth and put them in pole position for a long-awaited European adventure the following season. The Cottagers had not won at the Lane for more than half a century and, on the back of their convincing 4–1 dismantling of Sunderland last time out, hopes were high of three priceless points.

The first chance of the game fell to Teddy Sheringham after just four minutes and it was a gilt-edged one. Darren Anderton provided the cross from wide, Sheringham was unmarked but he somehow contrived to direct his free header wide of the mark. The miss seemed to galvanise Fulham and, after fifteen minutes, they were ahead in the most fortuitous circumstances. Portuguese forward Luis Boa Morte surged forward and crossed menacingly into the box. Ledley was well aware of the danger and was first to the ball, only to see his attempted clearance fly past Keller into his own goal. Many defenders before and since have suffered the same indignity, but the scoreboard still read Spurs 0 – Fulham 1.

At least Tottenham's – if not Ledley's – luck was about to change. As half-time approached, Simon Davies was sent clean through by Anderton. The Welsh international kept his cool as he rounded Maik Taylor in the Fulham goal but, just as it seemed he had to score, he was hauled down by the 'keeper. Referee Graham Barber immediately pointed to the spot and, as Taylor was the last line of the visitors' defence, he also showed him the red card. Sheringham stepped up to atone for his earlier glaring miss and Spurs were level.

They failed to capitalise on their numerical superiority in a strange second half that had chances at both ends and a second sending-off – this time Anderton headed for the dressing room prematurely after a second yellow. The game ended all square but it was not difficult to gauge which manager was happier with the stalemate at the final whistle. 'We had the break from Teddy's penalty and we should have gone on from there and won the game but, as it panned out, we went down to ten men,' Hoddle said. 'At half-time we said we mustn't switch off, but we didn't come out of the traps and be ruthless enough and that is where we ended up not winning the game.

'I thought we were laboured in our decision-making passing the ball. When you have an extra man, you have to make it pay. It was frustrating because we found ourselves chasing the game at 1–0. We slowly but surely started to play and get going – ending up with the penalty and them going down to ten men. With ten men behind the ball it was not going to be easy but, quite frankly, the boys didn't go out there and respond.'

Further disappointment was just around the corner in the shape of another London club and a familiar face. Spurs travelled to Upton Park to face the Hammers and lined up against Les Ferdinand, whom Hoddle had allowed to leave on a free transfer in the January transfer window. The football gods demanded that the popular striker score against his former club and they got their wish when the former England man drilled a low shot into the far corner on the half-hour mark. Future Spurs star Michael Carrick doubled the lead after the break and Tottenham's European ambitions had suffered a serious setback.

The quest for UEFA Cup football was not to become any easier. Liverpool were next up at the Lane and, fresh from beating arch rivals Manchester United in the Final of the League Cup at the Millennium Stadium, they were justifiably brimming with confidence.

The fixture had a special resonance for Ledley. His Spurs début had come against the Reds at Anfield back in May 1999 during the George Graham years. Since having been thrust into action following Mauricio Taricco's sending-off, he had matured into an established Premiership player and a full England international, but the memories of that watershed day on Merseyside as an 18-year-old had not diminished.

'Liverpool is a game that stands out quite a lot for me. I made my début at Anfield, came on and played left-back. It's always a big game and we need to get a win at the moment,' he told the club website. 'We all believe we should have done better in our last two games and Liverpool will be confident after winning the Worthington Cup Final. It will be a tough game but we're up for it. They are a good side but we've done well against them at White Hart Lane and we're looking to continue that, definitely.'

Spurs however had their own cause for optimism. Liverpool had been beaten in their previous four league visits to the Lane and had not won there for seven years. The big threat to that record was Michael Owen, who had scored four in his last five club appearances (including the Reds' second in the recent Cup Final victory) and Ledley was acutely aware of the need to shackle the England star. 'On his day, Michael is untouchable,' he admitted. 'He's so quick, great movement, and that is always hard to play against as a defender. He's a clever player with that pace as well, so that makes it doubly hard. It's a big challenge for me but I look forward to these games. These are the games any player wants to be involved in.'

Hoddle had a defensive headache before the game. Dean Richards was suspended and Chris Perry was still nursing a slipped disc in his neck, so he decided to revert to a 4-4-2 formation and partner Ledley with Ben Thatcher, normally a full-back, in the centre of the defence. Spurs' new-look centre-half pairing would have to stand strong.

Surprisingly for two teams with a reputation for attacking football, there were no goals in the first half but the players' half-time cuppas seemed to work miracles as both sides emerged in a more positive frame of mind and proceeded to conjure up five goals between them.

Unfortunately, three of them were to fall to the visitors.

Spurs took the lead in unlikely, almost comical fashion when Taricco picked up possession 25 yards out from the Liverpool goal and launched a speculative shot goalwards. Reds 'keeper Jerzy Dudek seemed to have the effort well covered, but inexplicably spilled the ball and it crept over the line. Tottenham were in front and Taricco had his first goal for the club, some five years after signing from Ipswich.

A mistake gifted Liverpool an equaliser just two minutes later when Teddy Sheringham fatally lost possession on the edge of the area and, with the Spurs defence flat-footed, Steven Gerrard whipped in a cross that Owen couldn't fail to poke into the net. The visitors went ahead when Emile Heskey headed home at the far post and, again, it came from another costly mistake – this time Kasey Keller throwing the ball straight to Jamie Carragher, who fed Gerrard who, in turn, all but placed the ball on Heskey's head. The game was done and dusted eight minutes from time when Gerrard spearheaded a Liverpool counter-attack and beat Keller from twenty yards. Sheringham gave the home crowd fleeting hope with Spurs' second with three minutes left on the clock but it was too little, too late and the points belonged to the Merseysiders.

Ledley had spoken in the pre-match build-up of the need to subdue Owen's predatory threat and, although the England star did score after a Spurs mistake, Ledley had done a magnificent job on the striker. Liverpool's second came from another unforced error and the third was a result of Tottenham having to throw bodies forward looking for the equaliser. Hoddle's side had conceded three but Ledley and Thatcher had been superb.

'There was nothing wrong with the performance, apart from throwing away the game,' the manager said. 'We were in control at 1–0 and gave two silly goals away. They were individual errors, no one means to make them but they've hurt us big time. We should have been able to hit them on the break but, very quickly, handed the momentum back to them by giving two stupid goals away.

'Heskey's goal was offside. I thought that from the bench and have watched it. It is a tight one but is offside and that has gone against us. It was a very frustrating day. We played well enough to have won the game and came out with nothing. My thoughts are of total frustration and disappointment.

Whatever the circumstances, a third consecutive league game without victory was not the kind of form that would take the club into Europe. The team was faltering alarmingly and Ledley seemed powerless to stop it. His personal performances remained commanding but there was no escaping the reality that they needed a dramatic upturn in form to threaten UEFA Cup qualification.

Club form dictates international selection. But so does the form of your team-mates and, as a defender, you will often be judged by the number of goals you concede collectively as a back four rather than on your individual performances. And so it was to be for Ledley.

After the débâcle against Australia, England's next assignment was a vital Euro 2004 qualifying double-header against Liechtenstein in Vaduz, followed four days later by the visit of Turkey to Sunderland's Stadium of Light. England had stuttered in their previous qualifier against Macedonia at St Mary's, only managing a disappointing draw, and two victories over the minnows of Liechtenstein and the difficult Turks were vital.

Although now capped twice, Ledley was yet to feature in a competitive game for his country and, when Eriksson announced his squad for the all-important games, it was obvious he would have to wait a bit longer. For the first time, Ledley had been overlooked while fully fit and it was the first major setback of his career to his international aspirations. He had been deemed, albeit temporarily, surplus to requirements.

Eriksson spoke only of the players he had selected for the games at his subsequent England press conferences but it was relatively easy to understand what had happened. The coach had picked five centre-halves – Rio Ferdinand, Sol Campbell and Gareth Southgate were automatic choices, but the two players who had leapfrogged Ledley in the pecking order were his old friend John Terry and Newcastle's highly-rated Jonathan Woodgate. Terry was still uncapped while Woodgate had four full England games under his belt.

There was little to choose between the trio in terms of experience. What was different was that Terry and Woodgate were both playing for club sides in good form. Both Chelsea and Newcastle were enjoying their best runs in recent seasons and their respective centre-halves enjoyed the reflected glow of that success. Spurs were hardly in freefall but Ledley was facing an uphill struggle. 'Naturally I'm disappointed at not making the England squad this time but I'm sure club form comes into it and maybe I've not been at my best,' he reasoned. 'We all know we've got to improve as a unit at Tottenham with our defending. We've got to put together a run where we are consistently keeping clean sheets.'

Bolton were next up at the Reebok and, for 90 minutes, it seemed Ledley would get his wish. Bolton huffed and puffed to break down the Spurs defence but they stood firm and, with the game into injury-time and still goalless, Tottenham were on course for a hard-earned point. But then disaster struck. French midfielder Youri Djorkaeff surged into the area and Gary Doherty lost his cool and hauled him down for a penalty. Djorkaeff dusted himself off and slotted home the resulting spot-kick and Spurs were left pointless and heartbroken.

The season was beginning to fall apart at the seams and anything but a victory over struggling Birmingham at White Hart Lane would be unthinkable. This time, however, it was Tottenham's turn to enjoy some good fortune.

The game kicked off with the Lane faithful doing their best to reinvigorate the team after their defeat at Bolton and the team responded accordingly, putting the Blues firmly on the back foot and, in the fifth minute, Hoddle's side enjoyed a crucial moment of good fortune. Birmingham goalkeeper Andy Marriott collected the ball in his area and dropped the ball at his feet ready to launch a clearance up field. He failed to notice Robbie Keane loitering with intent behind him and, as soon as the Irish marksman saw the ball hit the turf, he raced up, nicked the ball from under Marriott's nose and impudently passed the ball into the net. Marriott was left to rue what was probably the blunder of the season and Spurs were on their way.

Birmingham drew level with a 77th-minute penalty but Tottenham were not to be denied and Gus Poyet ensured the three points their performance deserved with a thunderous volley three minutes from time. The three-match losing run had been arrested and Hoddle was able celebrate this second anniversary as manager in style. 'We showed a lot of character and willingness to stick together,' a visibly relieved Hoddle said after the match. 'We kept going. We conceded another penalty and you are thinking, "Is it going against us again?" but the crowd stayed patient, got behind us and, in the end, it paid dividends.

'Gus made a great run and it was a superb one-touch finish. He's at his best when he's one-touch finishing and, as soon as it landed, I thought, "He's going to hit this... " and what a strike it was. I was pleased with the performance and the most important thing was the three points. We didn't get them luckily, we deserved the win, but it was good how we kept at it. The fans went home happy in the end.'

Spurs had emerged with the spoils despite a second successive penalty award against them and, if the players were feeling slightly victimised by referees after the Birmingham game, they must have been positively paranoid in the wake of the visit to Elland Road a week later.

Leeds were fresh from a 6–1 demolition of Charlton at the Valley and dominated the opening exchanges, taking a deserved lead on the half-hour mark courtesy of Australian striker Mark Viduka. Spurs hit back in three destructive minutes through Teddy Sheringham and Robbie Keane, against his old club, and, as the game drew on in the second-half, it appeared they would be heading back to north London with what could prove to be a season-defining victory. And then the side's penalty curse struck again. Harry Kewell was felled by Kasey Keller and Viduka dispatched the spot-kick to earn Leeds a draw.

It was another bitter pill to swallow and, although Ledley was keen to emphasis the positives after the game, the truth was that Spurs had been denied two points they desperately needed in their bid to finish in the top six. There were just five league games left in the season and the margin for error was diminishing with each game.

'Our last few performances haven't really been up to scratch and it was nice to come away from an away game thinking that we did play well and deserved something out of the game,' Ledley told the Spurs website. 'I thought they started off brightly but, once they took the lead, we played our best football of the game. For a little spell they couldn't really deal with us. We got our two goals and were a bit disappointed in the end that we couldn't hang on to it. It woke us up a bit but we settled down and played well.'

A defeat to Manchester City and a victory over relegated West Brom at the Hawthorns left Tottenham's hopes European competition hanging by the most fragile of threads and only victory over title-chasing Manchester United at the Lane would keep the dream alive. The club would still have to rely on other sides' results, but it would all be academic if they couldn't beat United.

'Everyone is going to be looking at the game and it is a chance for us to go for a big result after an indifferent couple of months,' Ledley said. 'It would be nice to get a result. There is a lot on the game. For them, they are obviously going for the league, while we are fighting for every point that we can at the moment to strengthen our place in the table. It should be a good game – it always is. These are the games you want to play in, where you can see how far you've come.'

The stakes were raised even further 24 hours before kick-off when Arsenal – United's title rivals – were held to a 2–2 draw at Bolton. United knew victory at Spurs would send them five points clear at the top of the table and they came out for the game with the air of a side intent on doing the business.

In truth, Tottenham were on the back foot throughout the match and if it had not been for another outstanding performance from Ledley and a succession of superb saves from Kasey Keller, the team could have suffered a humiliatingly heavy defeat. As it was, Paul Scholes and Ruud van Nistelrooy both struck to complete a 2–0 victory and sent United towards the Premiership title. Spurs, in stark contrast, were going nowhere.

Confirmation that the season was effectively over hit the players firmly between the eyes and they capitulated woefully in their final two games – going down 5–1 at the Riverside to Bolton before a 4–0 defeat at home to Blackburn. It was a dreadful way to sign off and, even though the summer promised a period in which to reflect and, hopefully, strengthen, those two results in particular were to have serious repercussions the following season.

The Blackburn match was doubly disappointing because it was Teddy Sheringham's final game for the club. In his second spell at White Hart Lane, the England striker had scored 125 goals in 277 appearances for Spurs and to bow out on the back of such an abject performance was hardly a fitting way to say goodbye. 'I really felt that we had the balance between young and old, between youth and experience,' Sheringham wrote in the Blackburn match programme. 'Sadly, that blend hasn't quite materialised.'

Unfortunately, he was absolutely right. Tottenham had limped home in 10th place and the early season optimism that had caught hold at the Lane had evaporated. Ledley had been blameless as the campaign collapsed around him but, after his battle to regain full fitness, his second England call-up and his frequent Man of the Match displays, he probably deserved more.

The Spurs players did not immediately scatter across the globe for their summer holidays in the sun. The club had been invited to face Major League soccer side DC United in the States and the team were forced to jet across the Atlantic to contest the grandly-named Capital Cup in Washington. The trip ended in a 1–0 defeat and, finally, the squad disbanded to reflect on the season, the alarming slump and what might or should have been.

A few months earlier, Ledley could have reasonably hoped to be spending his summer in an England shirt. The Football Association had organised friendlies against Serbia

& Montenegro at Leicester's Walkers Stadium and Slovakia at Middlesbrough's Riverside in early June, but Sven-Göran Eriksson was not yet ready to welcome him back into the international fold. Ledley, it seemed, was to set to ply his trade solely for his club for the foreseeable future.

Still only aged 22, it was far from a terminal snub from the England set-up. He had time on his side but, after experiencing international football so early in his career, it was impossible to forget the experience and he ached to force his way back into contention. England were blessed with a generation of top-quality centre-halves and Ledley had no option but to be patient.

His first priority had to be ending his pre-season jinx. The hip injury had devastated his previous summer's preparations, as well as denying Tottenham his services for the first three months of the campaign, and it was crucial that he avoided a repeat of his misfortune twelve months later.

Suitably sunned and rested, the players reported back for pre-season training in early July. The club were due to fly out for a prestigious tour of South Africa later in the month but, before they boarded the plane, there was the grind of the first two weeks back, the double training sessions and exhausting stamina work. Few players relish the monotony of endless fitness drills without a ball at their feet, but Ledley was simply happy to be involved at this stage.

'I feel a lot sharper and a lot more confident when I've done a proper pre-season,' he told the club website. 'Personally, I feel that I need pre-season to get me in shape and feeling at a peak. That brings confidence. Missing the previous summer definitely affected me.'

Before the team were scheduled to head off to South Africa, there were four domestic fixtures to contend with. The first was against Stevenage Borough at Broadhall Way and, as the first run-out of the new campaign, it was intended to be little more than a gentle practice match to ease the players back into the swing of things. Unfortunately, it didn't quit pan out like that for Ledley. The big defender was only meant to play the first half of the match as Glenn Hoddle changed his entire starting line-up for the second period, but during those fateful 45 minutes, Ledley managed to pick up a seemingly innocuous ankle injury that would once again decimate his pre-season preparations.

There were no real alarm bells when Ledley initially reported the niggle to the Spurs medical staff. It didn't seem to be a serious problem but friendly fixtures against Wycombe Wanderers, Oxford United and Norwich City came and went and Ledley was not ready to play. The squad then departed for South Africa for the games against the Orlando Pirates and the Kaiser Chiefs (not to mention a meeting with Archbishop Desmond Tutu) and the 22-year-old was forced to put away his passport and continue with the lonely work on his rehabilitation. The sense of déjà vu was inescapable.

While King was sidelined, Hoddle and the club board were busy reassessing the first-team squad that had proved just too threadbare the previous season. Teddy Sheringham was already on his way to West Ham on a

Bosman free and the manager now had to decide who was surplus to requirements. In the wake of Sheringham's emotional departure, he also needed to find a new club captain. 'There are things to be learned from last season and there are things to improve on,' Hoddle admitted during the preseason build-up. He admitted that the team had given too many goals away, and that the injury list hadn't helped. With one or two key players back to relative fitness (Ziege and Redknapp), Hoddle felt that it was vital to keep them out of harm's way, but needed them to move towards their peak at the beginning of the season. He also hoped that the right sort of activity in the transfer market over the summer would strengthen the squad enormously, and enable the team to compete at a higher level. For success to be enjoyed, though, the injuries could not continue in the way they had done the previous season. If that was avoided, then Hoddle believed 'we can turn it around and get success for Tottenham. I am determined to do that.'

The clear-out began in earnest in mid-July when Ben Thatcher was allowed to sign for Leicester on a free. Steffen Freund, Steffen Iversen, Matthew Etherington and Neil Sutton had all followed him out of the door by the end of August and Hoddle turned his attentions to bringing new faces in. Brighton striker Bobby Zamora was the first to arrive and, over the course of the summer, he was joined by West Ham duo Freddie Kanouté and Jermain Defoe, Sheffield United Michael Brown and Fulham midfielder and Ledley's former Under-21 team-mate Sean Davis. In total, Spurs spent over £15 million in the transfer market and now only time would tell whether the club had signed the right players.

The captaincy was a moot point because there were was no clear-cut candidate. The elder statesmen Gus Poyet and Jamie Redknapp had the prerequisite experience but there were question marks about the number of games both would play in terms of fitness and stamina for the forthcoming season. Dean Richards was another possibility, but many supporters believed that even at the tender age of 22, Ledley was a genuine contender. He would have been the first to concede he wasn't the most vocal or accomplished communicator in the team, but his consistency, calm authority and apprenticeship through the club's junior ranks could not be discounted. In the end, Hoddle handed the armband to Redknapp and, although he may have had little idea at time, Ledley would not have to wait too much longer for his chance to lead Tottenham out.

Spurs' pre-season continued after their South African sojourn with two high-profile games at the Lane against PSV Eindhoven and Sporting Lisbon. They were the climax of Hoddle's preparations for the new Premiership campaign and, although Ledley's recovery from the ankle injury was going well, he still wasn't ready to return to action. The nightmare scenario had materialised and Tottenham would have to begin the season without their inspirational centre-half.

The first league game took Hoddle's side to St Andrews to face Steve Bruce's Birmingham City, but hopes of a winning start were dashed by David Dunn's first-half free kick. Spurs mounted a concerted second-half fightback but there was no way through the home defence and they came away empty-handed.

Thankfully there was good news just around the corner. Three days later, Ledley and fellow centre-half Dean Richards, who been nursing an Achilles injury, were ready to return to action and both were named in the reserve-team game against Portsmouth. If both came through unscathed, it would be a massive boost to their manager.

'I've been training since the end of the last week towards a specific game that I've been aiming for – the reserve game tonight,' he told the club website. 'At the moment, the ankle is feeling good and I'm feeling quite good in training. I just want to get this game under my belt and hopefully try and push on from there.

'I think I just went over on it against Stevenage. It was a bit sore during the game but one of those where you can get through to half-time, which is what I wanted to do. I was in a bit of pain after the game and it seemed to drag on from there. It was a little sprain of the ligaments – it wasn't too bad. I've been to Germany to see a doctor out there and he helped a lot.'

Hoddle must have been more than a little nervous watching two such influential first-teamers testing their injuries for the first time in weeks, but his luck was about to change and the pair both played the full 90 minutes without incident. Hoddle's selection options had suddenly increased and the manager had little hesitation in naming both of them in his starting line-up to face Leeds United at the Lane. The Yorkshire side had been ravaged by a financial crisis which had precipitated the sale of many of their leading lights, but Ledley was adamant Tottenham could ill afford to assume they would be a soft touch in north London.

'They've lost a lot of players but, at the moment, they still have a few great players in their squad. They always provide a tough game and they are a good fighting side. You can never underestimate them, but they could have been challenging for titles now if they hadn't lost players. [Mark] Viduka and [Alan] Smith are two quality strikers and any defenders are in for a tough game against them.'

Fight is exactly what Spurs had to do in front of an expectant home crowd of almost 35,000 after going behind to Smith's fifth-minute opener. But they refused to panic and were back on level terms before half-time when Mauricio Taricco showed superb individual skills, skipped past two tackles and unleashed a fierce shot that rippled the back of the net.

The fans were baying for more in the second 45 minutes and got exactly what they demanded. Hoddle hauled off Bobby Zamora on the hour to give Freddie Kanouté his Spurs début and, just ten minutes later, the Frenchman repaid the first instalment of his £4.4 million summer transfer fee with a stunning overhead kick to put his new team in the lead. Tottenham were determined to hang on and, when the final whistle came, the three points were safe.

After the match, Hoddle admitted he had taken a risk playing both Ledley and Richards after their disrupted pre-seasons, but his delight at the first win of the season was evident. 'Deano and Ledley deserve a pat on the back because 90 minutes of reserve football in the whole of pre-season isn't enough,' he said. 'We took a chance and they responded. They played exceedingly well. I can't remember a Leeds chance after the goal and we should have done better on that. Credit to them and Anthony Gardner. We looked solid and there wasn't a player out there who didn't play a part.'

Confidence restored, Spurs began to prepare for the testing trip to Merseyside to face Liverpool. Tottenham had not come away from Anfield with even a single league point, let alone three, since 1996 and the game would be a severe examination of Ledley, Richards and Anthony Gardener, whom Hoddle had selected as his back three.

The home side were undeniably the more potent of the two sides going forward but it wasn't until the 72nd minute that Kasey Keller was genuinely tested in the Spurs goal when he denied Steven Gerrard and Tottenham hung on for a goalless draw. Hoddle's side appeared to have found the defensive solidity that had all too frequently eluded them the previous season.

'We came here to get three points but defended very well,' Hoddle enthused after the match. 'That's the first time since I've been here as manager that I've been able to play that back three for the second game on the trot. Someone has always been injured, suspended, whatever. We looked solid and they found it hard to break us down.

'Credit to Ledley and Dean... they've not had a pre-season and they've been thrown in at the deep end and responded. If we can get one more game out of them on Saturday then we'll have two weeks where we can get some sharp training down them and they'll be better for that. Credit to them, we defended well as a team. We were solid but had enough possession and deserved the point we got here.'

It didn't last. Fulham were the next opponents three days later and arrived looking for their first win at White Hart Lane since 1948. Few expected them to get it, but the Cottagers clearly hadn't read the script. Tottenham enjoyed the better of the opening exchanges but Fulham took the lead midway through the half through Barry Hayles. Ledley had a great opportunity to level the match from Stephen Carr's right-footed corner but watched in disbelief as Dutch 'keeper Edwin van der Sar beat his side-footed effort away. It already seemed it might not be Spurs' day.

At half-time, Hoddle decided to make changes and there was a real sense of disbelief in the crowd when the team came out for the second period. Striker Bobby Zamora was off the bench in a bid to give the side more teeth going forward but the manager had taken Ledley off to accommodate him. It was a gamble in more ways than one. Spurs were only one down but Hoddle had decided to show his hand at the break rather than waiting to see how the first 15 minutes of the second-half played out. More significantly, he had hauled off the fans' favourite and that was not a popular decision.

The gamble backfired. Rather than giving Tottenham the impetus to retrieve the game, it made them vulnerable at the back and Fulham helped themselves to two more goals from Hayles and Luis Boa Morte. Spurs were beaten

3–0 on their own ground, and the Lane faithful made their feelings chillingly clear as they poured out of the stadium long before the final whistle. Of course, Ledley refused to criticise publicly his under-fire manager. It was the first time in his career he had been substituted for tactical reasons and, however much the decision must have stung, he kept his own counsel.

It was perhaps for the best that the team's next game – the London derby against Chelsea at Stamford Bridge – was two weeks away. It would let the dust settle on what was a disastrous result against Fulham and allow the manager and the players to assess what had gone so badly wrong and, hopefully, put it right.

The brief hiatus also gave Hoddle time to add two more players to his squad and he brought in French midfielder Stephane Dalmat from Inter Milan and left-back Paul Konchesky from Charlton. Both were loan deals and the latter meant a face from Ledley's past was once again a team-mate. Konchesky was another product of the seemingly endless Senrab production line and Ledley was delighted to have his old friend in the Tottenham fold.

'Paul's another one to make it from Senrab,' he told the club website. 'He was more of an attacking player back in those days and he used to play up front or down the left side. He's a very good player. He can play left-back or wing-back, he's quick, has a great left foot and I think he'll do well here. I think he just wants to push on and aid his own England chances. This will be a good place for him to do that.'

Konchesky was on the Spurs bench for the Chelsea game. Despite his shock substitution a fortnight ago,

Ledley was in the starting line-up but, once again, he did not make it past half-time. Unfortunately this time, his absence after the break at Stamford Bridge was not tactical and he was forced off with a hamstring injury in the 39th minute. His return from the pre-season injury had lasted just four games.

Without Ledley in the middle of the defence, Spurs looked increasingly vulnerable and, despite a brace from Freddie Kanouté, they were outplayed and Chelsea's crushing 4–2 win extended the Blues' unbeaten league run over their London rivals to 27 games. Hoddle was now firmly in the firing line and the odds on him being sacked tumbled.

These were dark days at Spurs. The media smelt blood in the water and speculated about Hoddle's future on an almost daily basis. On the pitch, the team had suffered two desperate defeats in succession and now Ledley was sidelined with his hamstring problem and was already ruled out of the next game – Southampton at White Hart Lane.

It was an ironic twist of fate that it had to be the Saints next up, Hoddle's previous club. His job was in real jeopardy; defeat at home could spell the end of his Tottenham tenure and the team which he had left more than two years ago were now in the position to administer the last rites.

Despite the recent turmoil and disastrous results, the Spurs fans chose to roar the team on to the pitch against Southampton, but the cacophony of noise was silenced after just three minutes when James Beattie headed the opener from a corner. The sense of expectation and hope had turned to despair in an instant and there was to be no way back for the home side. Beattie added the second minutes before half-time and Kevin Phillips helped himself to the third on the hour. Freddie Kanouté did get Spurs on the score sheet but it was not even a consolation. It was a second successive home defeat with three goals conceded and Hoddle probably knew it was all over.

The club confirmed the inevitable the day after the Southampton disaster – Hoddle had been sacked. 'Following two seasons of disappointing results, there was a significant investment in the team during the summer, in order to give us the best possible chance of success this season,' Spurs chairman Daniel Levy said in a statement.

'Unfortunately, the start to this season has been our worst since the Premiership was formed. Coupled with the extremely poor second half to last season, the current lack of progress and any visible sign of improvement are unacceptable. It is critical that I, and the board, have absolute confidence in the manager to deliver success to the club. Regrettably, we do not. It is not a decision we have taken lightly. However, we are determined to see this club succeed and we must now move forward.

'Glenn occupies a special place at this club. Today's decision in no way detracts from the fact that he was one of our greatest players. He will always be welcome at White Hart Lane. I should like to thank him personally for his determination and commitment and wish him well. We shall be thorough in our search for a new manager. It is a crucial appointment and we shall take the time necessary to make the best choice.'

The decision to sack one of the Lane's favourite sons was an unpalatable one for all concerned. Hoddle's appointment had been greeted with widespread enthusiasm but the stark reality was that the team had not moved significantly forward during his reign in terms of league position or consistency of results. Spurs had won just 41 of 104 games under his leadership and his side's spectacular implosion at the end of the previous season – winning just one of their final six games to throw away the chance of European football – coupled with a disastrous start to the new campaign, had meant that the writing was on the wall.

Hoddle was understandably devastated by the news. 'I am shocked and disappointed to have parted company with Tottenham over the weekend only six matches into the new season,' he said. 'This is the first time in my managerial career it has happened to me for football reasons.

'I have been a dedicated professional and also a lifelong Spurs fan, and no one could have tried harder to turn things round for the club. I have built a great squad that, when fully fit, can go on to do very well this season. I feel sure this turning point will happen very soon.

'I particularly want to thank the Spurs fans who have shown me great support and loyalty from the beginning right to the end. I really wanted to return Spurs to the glory days for the fans. I wish the players and the club every success for the future.'

For Ledley, Hoddle's departure was a blow. He was the coach who had made him the lynchpin of the Tottenham defence, ending George Graham's experiment of deploying him in midfield and, under Hoddle's tutelage, Ledley had become a full England player. The uncertainty following his sacking would not benefit any of the Spurs players.

As soon as the news broke, the speculation about Hoddle's replacement began in earnest. According to the press, Rangers' Alex McLeish, Celtic's Martin O'Neill, Harry Redknapp at Portsmouth, Charlton's Alan Curbishley and Graeme Souness at Blackburn were the front-runners for the vacant position. In the end, however, the club decided to look closer to home and opted to install Director of Football David Pleat as caretaker manager with Chris Hughton promoted to first-team coach.

Pleat was certainly a familiar face in the hot seat. He had managed the club between May 1986 and October 1987 and he had also stepped into the breach as caretaker boss on two previous occasions. If Spurs were looking for some reassuring continuity, they had chosen the right man.

There was little time from him to ease himself back into the role. Tottenham faced a second-round League Cup clash at Coventry City just three days after Hoddle's exit and the team were in desperate need of a result. 'We've just got to try to stabilise things as the players will have all sorts of thoughts going through their heads,' Pleat admitted in his pre-match interview with the Tottenham website. 'We've just got to be positive and get back on the winning trail, which breeds confidence. We'll pull through it... decisions have been made and the club has got to go on and be strong.

'We will all focus our minds on the immediate future. There is no future in the past – that is sad, but true. Every game is important. We want to win games and would like to have a League Cup run… we want to get up the league – we want to do all the things that the supporters want for us. It will take a big effort by everyone, everyone has to be true to themselves and I'm sure we can improve things.'

In time-honoured football tradition, the recent upheaval, the loss of their manager and the appointment of a new coach served to galvanise the team and goals from Kanouté, Robbie Keane and youngster Rohan Ricketts guided Spurs to a morale-boosting 3–0 victory. A draw at Manchester City, followed by a win over Everton, went a long way to lifting much of the gloom that had settled over White Hart Lane, and the news that Ledley was poised to return to the first team after shaking off his hamstring injury only added to the sense of relief and renewed hope.

His enforced lay-off had been a bizarre time for the player. While he was on the treatment table, the club had sacked the manager and Ledley had celebrated his 23rd birthday. His last appearance against Chelsea had been his 99th for Spurs and he had been forced to wait patiently to make it a century of first-team games. The good news was that he was almost ready to play again.

'It's coming along as planned really and, hopefully, I should be training next week,' he said at the start of October. 'I think I'll have to wait until after the international break and it will give me a chance to make sure I get some good training under my belt before my next game.' Ledley added that the hamstring tear had been minor, and that he'd been to Germany a few times to have it examined by one of the world's specialists. He was due to start ball work within a week, and had already started some light running exercises.

The international break saw England held to a goalless draw against Turkey in Istanbul in mid-October. David Beckham dramatically missed a penalty late on but the point was enough to confirm Sven-Göran Eriksson's side as Group Seven winners and book their place in the Euro 2004 finals in Portugal the following summer. Having missed out on selection for the World Cup in 2002, Ledley now had the incentive of another major finals to aim for.

He was not, however, fully fit for the next Premiership game after the qualifier – a 2–1 triumph at the Walkers Stadium over Leicester City – but the hamstring had healed sufficiently for Pleat to name him among his substitutes for the visit of Middlesbrough to the Lane seven days later.

It was a fiercely-contested but ultimately scrappy encounter and Ledley watched the first 68 minutes of the game unfold from the warmth of the bench, until Pleat decided to make a tactical change. Gus Poyet was taken off, whereupon Ledley was thrown into the holding role in midfield and the boy from Bow made his 100th appearance for the club. The remainder of the game was largely uneventful, but for Leadley, the milestone in his career meant the world. He was now back in the team with a century of games under his belt.

It was also his first game for Pleat in his latest spell as caretaker manager and it seemed the new boss had fresh

edley gave a typically calm and self-assured performance during England's 3–0 defeat Ukraine at St James' Park in April 2004.

© *PA Photos*

Top left: The Ernst Happel Stadium in Vienna was packed with over 45,000 Austrian far for England's Group Six fixture in September 2004. Nevertheless, Ledley's first 60 minutes were some of the most comfortable of his career to date. © *Sportbeat Imag*

Top middle: Winning the ball ahead of Portugal's Pedro Miguel Pauleta during a friendl in February 2002. © *PA Pho*

Bottom: After a seven-month absence, Ledley won his 17th England cap in October 200 against Macedonia, as well as Man of the Match. He is pictured here poised to take the ball from Goran Pandev. © *Clevamed*

Top right: At the crucial Euro 2008 decider the following June in Tallin against Estonia, Ledley's play was hailed as assured and commanding by his critics. © *Sportsbeat Imag*

p: The high-profile friendly against Brazil in June 2007 was England's first match at e rebuilt Wembley Stadium. Ledley was instrumental in repelling the visitors' first-half acks, though outfooted by Kaka in the second period. © *Clevamedia*

ottom: Organising an England wall with Gerrard, Lampard and Beckham. © *Clevamedia*

With the best years still ahead of him, Ledley King's talent and determination ensure h
is destined for even greater success.

ideas about Ledley's best position. George Graham had always seen him as a destructive, holding midfielder, while Hoddle was convinced of his qualities as a central defender. Under Pleat, it seemed the wheel had turned full circle and he was to be deployed as a shield for the back four.

'He did a very good job there,' Pleat explained after the game when asked why he had brought him on in midfield. 'He played a very steady, sensible passing game. He is a person that doesn't just kick the ball, he passes it and we needed someone to be calm and pass the ball.'

As ever, Ledley himself was diplomacy personified when he was asked what he made of his new role. Doubtless, the media were hoping he would break ranks and voice his displeasure at being 'played out of position', but they would get no joy from him. The 23-year-old was simply happy to be back in the team and didn't care where he was asked to play.

'Every game is going to help me get my fitness back and, obviously, I will get more used to the position the more games I play,' he said. 'At the moment, I am still trying to find my feet.

My responsibility is to provide a bit of protection for the back four I think. To break up play, hopefully, and give the ball simply. It can be difficult at times, but that is what I am there for, to help the team. If we are on the attack, my job is to get up the pitch and try and support our play.'

Whatever his private thoughts, he had done enough in his brief cameo against Middlesbrough to convince Pleat he was now ready for a full 90 minutes and the manager decided to start with him in a midfield quartet of Stephane Dalmat, Christian Ziege and Rohan Ricketts against West Ham in a League Cup third-round clash.

Fresh from their confidence-boosting clean sheet against 'Boro, Spurs looked comfortable at the back against their Nationwide opponents and, with Ledley lurking with intent whenever the Hammers threatened to launch a foray into the final third of the pitch, it seemed a formality that the home side would progress. The only problem was that they could not find a way through at the other end and, deep into the second-half, the game was still deadlocked. The dreaded extra-time loomed large, and then penalties, and when referee Graham Barber blew for the end of the 90 minutes, the result hung in the balance.

It was Ledley's first full match back but his natural stamina allowed him to carry on into extra time. Tottenham had not succeeded in piercing the West Ham defence in normal time but, after just two minutes of the additional 30, they scored. Bobby Zamora collected the ball on the edge of the area, spun and unleashed a low drive that beat David James in the corner. It was his first goal for the club in nine games following his £1.5 million switch from Brighton, and Spurs were through.

Over the next two months, Ledley slowly but surely worked his way back to his best. His match fitness returned quickly and his sharpness was not far behind, but Spurs' fortunes under Pleat fluctuated as much as they had done under Hoddle. Defeat in the north London derby at Highbury was followed by a face-saving victory over Aston Villa. An eye-catching 3–1 victory over Manchester City and a headline-grabbing 5–2 mauling of Wolves were quickly followed by a 4–0 capitulation to Newcastle at St James's Park. A diabolical 4–3 surrender to ten-man City in the FA Cup in February, having led by three goals, was partially forgotten three days later when Portsmouth were despatched 4–3 at White Hart Lane. Tottenham, in short, were invariably a good team to watch but their Jekyll and Hyde form persisted.

Pleat persisted with the Ledley experiment in midfield and his influence was growing by the match. 'I think I am getting a bit more comfortable in it,' he admitted. 'I always said that it would take a bit of time to adapt and, game by game, I am feeling a bit more comfortable. I'm in there mainly to try and break up the play if someone is playing in the hole or dropping off the front and give the simple ball to players that can do damage at the other end.

'If there is a chance for me to get forward, the manager has said it is not always about someone like Gus [Poyet] getting up there and we can rotate a little bit. It's nice to get the chance to go forward and see what you can create for the team. I haven't scored for ages so I've forgotten what that feeling is like.'

He rediscovered his scoring touch in the 4–2 win over Charlton at the Valley in February and with Sven-Göran Eriksson set to announce his squad for a friendly in Portugal just days later, it was a timely reminder to the England coach that Ledley was on top of his game, albeit in midfield rather than the heart of the defence.

The question was whether Eriksson would pay any

attention. Although Ledley had missed a month of action earlier in the season – costing him his chance to force his way back into contention for the crucial Turkey match – the England coach had overlooked him for a friendly against Denmark in November even though he was back to full fitness. The Euro 2004 clock was inexorably counting down and Ledley's chances of making the European Championships in Portugal were hanging in the balance.

5

EUROPEAN MISADVENTURE

At the age of 23, Ledley King had arguably experienced more highs and lows in his still embryonic career than some fellow professionals might during their entire playing days. His senior début had come at the amphitheatre of football that is Anfield at the tender age of 18, he had played for his country by the age of 21 and he was widely regarded as the heartbeat of his club side.

On the negative side, he'd already spent a disproportionate amount of time on the treatment table for such a young and physically strong player. He had over a one hundred top-flight appearances to his name – no mean feat for any 23-year-old player – but it would have been so many more had it not been for a series of niggling injuries and frustrating setbacks.

In short, the six years since he signed his first

professional contract with Tottenham had been a roller-coaster ride. The next six months, though, were to eclipse everything that had come before.

England had safely negotiated their Euro 2004 qualifying campaign and Sven-Göran Eriksson could now turn his thoughts to the players he would select for the finals in Portugal in the summer. England would play four more games before heading to the Iberian peninsula for the finals in June and, although, as ever, in the build-up to a major international tournament, some players were already cast-iron certainties for the squad, there were still places up for grabs. It was now Eriksson's task to sort the wheat from the chaff before announcing who would spearhead England's challenge.

His first opportunity to run the rule over his options away from the pressure cooker atmosphere of the qualifying games themselves had come back in November in the friendly against Denmark at Old Trafford. He had ignored Ledley's claims for that match but now a game with Portugal in Faro loomed – just four short months before the finals proper – and everyone knew his squad for the Portuguese foray would provide a real insight into the Swede's selection thoughts.

Ledley did not initially make the squad. Even with centre-halves Rio Ferdinand and Jonathan Woodgate ruled out by injury, Eriksson chose to recall Middlesbrough veteran Gareth Southgate, as cover for John Terry, and Sol Campbell. Ledley's prospects appeared distinctly bleak and, if he had taken time to listen to one of Eriksson's pre-match press conferences, he would have been forgiven for heading to the nearest travel agents and booking his summer holiday there and then.

'It's a pity that Woodgate is injured. He's very unlucky. He's doing very well but every time we play, he is injured,' Eriksson explained when asked about his defensive options. 'I'm sure that any club or national team would miss Rio Ferdinand. I think he was the best or at least one of the best central defenders at the World Cup two years ago. He played in all the games and was fantastic. So, of course, if you don't have players like that, you miss them on the pitch.

'I think it's a nice race between Terry and Woodgate to show me who's going to play. There will be others as well but from what I see today, it's going to be one of those two. Southgate is playing well, he's another one. As for young players, there is [Anthony] Gardner – who's injured now I think – Zat Knight and Wes Brown.'

Ledley's name was conspicuous by its absence from Eriksson's comments and the Spurs star appeared to be completely off the international radar. And then fate intervened and, for once in his career, injuries were to work in his favour.

Two days after Eriksson announced his squad for the Portugal game, Sol Campbell and John Terry were both forced to withdraw with niggling injuries and, despite having failed to mention him in his earlier press conference, the Swede decided to call up Ledley. It was an overdue slice of luck and would prove to be a pivotal point in his whole career.

'Ledley is a good young player,' Eriksson told the

Football Association website. 'I have seen him play several times this season. He is strong and skilful and can play in many positions. It will be good to have him with us.

'We're a bit unlucky to be without four extremely good central defenders – not only in England – but the world. But it will be good to see other players. I think Ledley is ready – but we will see.'

When the time came to finalise his starting XI, Eriksson made good on his words and named Ledley in the heart of his defence alongside Southgate. Just a few days earlier, it seemed that he was on the international scrapheap at the age of 23 and now he was to make his first start for his country and win a third cap. It was an incredible turnaround of fortunes for the Spurs man.

On the morning of the game, Henry Winter wrote in the *Daily Telegraph*, 'If Ledley King, in for the injured John Terry alongside Gareth Southgate, springs a surprise and proves to the manor born at centre-half, the match will prove worthwhile.'

His selection at centre-half did not worry Ledley in the slightest, despite having spent most of the season in the Tottenham midfield. The step up from club to international football is notoriously difficult, but even more so when asked to play in a different position, but Ledley's versatility meant he was more than confident in his ability to revert to the back four against Portugal at the Estadio Algarve.

'I was always a central defender but then George Graham tried me in midfield for a little spell,' he said. 'After that, I went back into the defence but this season I was injured and the only way I could get back into the team was in midfield because it was going well at the back at the time. David Pleat asked me to play there and I have been happy to do so as long as I am enjoying it.

Ledley still considered himself a defender, though, and felt that that was where he had the best chance of playing for England. He was all the more surprised, therefore, that the call-up had been while he'd been playing in midfield for his club. Interestingly, Ledley remembered that John Terry had also been a noted midfielder for Senrab, adding that, even then, Terry had displayed leadership potential.

The match was played in front of 27,000 fans in Faro and it was the home side who started more brightly. Portuguese legend Luis Figo was playing his 100th game for his country and he almost marked the emotional occasion with a fairytale goal after five minutes. Simao crossed from the left, Ashley Cole failed to get sufficient distance on his clearing header and Figo powered in a fizzing shot that David James did well to keep out. England had been warned.

The Portuguese looked slick and dangerous on the ball and Ledley and the rest of the defence had to be on their toes. England had their own chances at the other end but Wayne Rooney was unable to get a touch on Michael Owen's cross, while Owen, in turn, was unable to make the most of Paul Scholes' chipped pass and the two teams went in at half-time all square.

Eriksson resisted the temptation to make a slew of half-times changes as he had done in previous friendly encounters, reflecting the importance of the game in terms of his Euro 2004 preparations. Joe Cole, Kieron Dyer and Danny Mills came on for Frank Lampard, Paul Scholes and Gary Neville respectively but, beyond that, the England coach was content to leave things unchanged.

The second-half was only two minutes old when England struck. David Beckham took a free-kick from the edge of the area and his delivery caused panic in the Portugal defence, who were unable to clear. Ledley was lurking with intent at the far post and made the most of the indecision to bundle the ball home. He had his first international goal and England were in front.

The remainder of the match was frenetic with chances at both ends. Portugal almost had an instant equaliser when James spilled the ball in his area under no pressure and was rescued by Southgate, while England almost doubled their advantage when Wayne Bridge fired across the face of goal.

Portugal controversially drew level after 70 minutes. Nicky Butt was pulled up for a challenge on Luis Boa Morte, even though Deco appeared to have handled the ball and, from the resulting free-kick, Pauleta stepped up and unleashed an unstoppable shot that rocketed into the top corner. There was one final chance when Portugal 'keeper Ricardo stopped Joe Cole's goal-bound effort with his legs, but the final whistle ended the contest and it was honours even in Faro.

It had been a great game from the Spurs man. An important goal and a commanding defensive display were all he could have hoped for and there was widespread acknowledgement of his performance in the press the following day. 'King, who had previously made two substitute appearances for his country, refused to be intimidated by the pace of Portugal,' the *Evening Standard* reported. 'He made timely interceptions, good block tackles and was a powerful presence in the air.' The verdict from the *Independent* was equally effusive: 'Eriksson will also have noted the performance of Ledley King, who played with a maturity which belied his inexperience and suggested he is capable of gatecrashing the European Championships.'

Eriksson himself was also a happy man. Ledley's display gave him a pleasant selection problem and, after his late call-up to the squad, the decision to throw him into the starting line-up now looked like a tactical masterstroke.

'We were playing away against Portugal, who are one of the favourites for Euro 2004, and we did very well in the first and second halves,' the England coach said after the game. 'If I have to talk about individuals, then the first I would like to pick out is Ledley King... he put in an excellent performance. It showed he is ready for the big international games, even though he was in a position he has not played for a while. He played a part in the goal as well. I learned that Ledley King is ready. He had an excellent performance, was not nervous at all and his defensive play was very good. He's much closer to it now, though much will depend on who is available. He came into the squad very late and I couldn't have expected a performance like that – with a goal as well. We haven't played for three months and it's very good to come together.'

The universal plaudits for Ledley's performance in the Algarve were obviously music to his ears but they also gave the young defender food for thought. Before the Portugal game, he had always ostensibly been happy to play for club or country in whatever role he was asked to fill, but it was now beginning to dawn on him that his international aspirations would be best served if he began to shed his reputation as 'Mr Versatile'. Injuries had worked in his favour prior to the Portugal game, but he could not rely on the same set of circumstances in the future. He needed to nail his positional colours to the mast.

'It shows Sven's got faith in me by calling me up,' he said. 'Maybe I'll have to talk to David Pleat about my role. I enjoy playing in midfield but, to get the best out of me, it may be something I'll have to look at. I was quite nervous coming into the game. If it didn't show, that's a good thing.'

Tellingly, Ledley admitted, 'If I'm going to get on to the squad, it will be as a defender... I don't feel I'm good enough in a midfield position.' He was clearly becoming more and more convinced of his natural attributes as a central defender, and now wanted others to take note. And if his England career depended on it, then Ledley was going to do all he could to give himself the best shot of becoming a permanent member of the squad.

Back at White Hart Lane, Ledley's task was to ensure that his form was good enough to keep him in Eriksson's thoughts. The next England game was a friendly with Sweden in Gothenburg in March and, although Pleat persisted with him in midfield, it was still crucial he maintained the quality the England manager was looking for.

There was, however, one off-field distraction that needed to be dealt with. His elevation to the England team and the possibility of him showcasing his talents on the big stage at Euro 2004 had made Spurs nervous. Ledley's contract ran out in the summer of 2005 and they feared other clubs would try to court their star player. The memories of Sol Campbell leaving on a Bosman free were still painfully fresh and the board was eager to get him to put pen to paper on a new, long-term deal.

The player and his agent had already agreed a new £15,000 per week, five-year deal but, until February, it remained unsigned. It was an unnecessary distraction for the player and there were almost audible sighs of relief around the Lane at the end of month when Ledley committed himself to the club until 2009.

'We are delighted that Ledley has made this commitment,' David Pleat admitted when the announcement was made. 'He can be an important part of what we hope will be a vibrant and improving team. His attitude to both training and playing is a coach's dream and he is performing very well for us.'

Ledley echoed his manager's thoughts and stressed that he was convinced the club would go from strength to strength in the future. 'I had 18 months left of my existing deal; the club came to me and offered a new deal and I was happy to sign,' he told the Tottenham website. 'It's great to get it all done and dusted. We've a lot of good, young players at the club and I feel part of it here, so I see no reason to be looking elsewhere. I feel, with the players we've got, that the next couple of seasons could be exciting. We all want to get into Europe and I'm sure that's going to happen sooner rather than later.'

On the pitch, the chances of UEFA Cup qualification suffered a series of setbacks with defeats to Middlesbrough and Manchester United, but there would be more encouraging news just around the corner. Eriksson had named his squad to face Denmark and, this time, there would no late call-ups for Ledley. On the back of his display against Portugal, he was included from the start and, as Spurs travelled to the south coast to face Southampton, he could look forward to another opportunity at international level and a further chance to cement his place at Euro 2004.

The game at St Mary's went to Saints 1–0 and, although he played the full 90 minutes, Ledley's injury jinx struck again when it was confirmed after the game that he was suffering from a recurrence of his hamstring problems. There was no option but to pull out of the England squad. 'I have to be sensible and the hamstring is not right at the moment,' Ledley said, adding that he had to rest for a week at least, and then see how far he could contribute to the final league games for Tottenham. He had to hope that he could still impress in those last few games.

Once again, just as he seemed to be establishing himself in the international set-up, he was denied the chance to build on his good work. To make matters worse, the Denmark game was the last match before the summer. England had two games in early June against Japan and

Iceland for Eriksson to fine-tune his preparations, but if Ledley was to work his way back into the squad, he would have to convince the England coach on the strength of his form for Spurs.

Thankfully, the hamstring settled down quickly and he was back in the side for the next match – a 1–0 defeat by Chelsea at the Lane – but, worryingly, he was only fit enough to feature in four of the club's final seven league games. The memories of the Portugal game were beginning to fade and his involvement at Euro 2004 was now firmly in the balance.

Eriksson named his squad to tackle the Japanese and Iceland in the two warm-up games in mid-May, two days after the end of the Premiership season and, despite his staccato end to the campaign, the England coach kept faith with Ledley. He would have his chance to impress and, with the final Euro 2004 squad announced at the start of June, there was still time to make himself indispensable.

The clash with Japan at the City of Manchester Stadium saw Ledley get a meagre two minutes on the pitch when he substituted for John Terry late on, but he was to play 45 minutes in the 6–1 demolition of Iceland four days later and was unlucky not to get his second international goal when his powerful header was cleared off the line by Toddy Gudjonsson. More significantly, England kept a clean sheet in the second half with Ledley and Jamie Carragher in the middle of the back four and, while he hadn't had enough time to settle any lingering doubts about his selection, he had done his cause no harm at all.

June was to be a momentous month in both Ledley's personal and professional life. It began with the news he had been praying for. Eriksson unveiled his squad for Euro 2004 and he was on his way to Portugal. He had been robbed of the chance to play in the World Cup two years earlier by injury, but now he would have the opportunity to showcase his talents on the international stage.

Back at White Hart Lane, meanwhile, there were was also news. The club had limped home to 14th place in the league – the team's lowest finish since 1998 – and the board decided that it was time to draw a line under David Pleat's tenure as caretaker manager. Ledley would return to the club after the European Championships to play for a new manager and that man would be France manager Jacques Santini, who had agreed to take the Spurs job after Euro 2004, and he had high hopes for the future in N17.

'I am delighted to get the opportunity to join Tottenham Hotspur,' the Frenchman said. 'I am an ambitious man and it has always been a dream of mine to coach a big English club in the most exciting league in the world. Tottenham Hotspur are a very big club, with a wonderful history and great traditions. Daniel [Levy] and Frank [Arnesen] have outlined their vision and I share their ambitions. I am determined to help the club return to its place amongst the élite and look forward to joining after Euro 2004.'

It was the high-profile appointment the Spurs fans had been longing for. The sense of uncertainty generated by Pleat's caretaker tenure was over and, with young players like Ledley having now served their top-flight apprenticeships, there was renewed optimism around the Lane.

Santini, however, would have to wait. England were now in Portugal for the finals and Ledley and the rest of the squad were looking ahead to their opener against defending champions France at the Estadio Da Luz in Lisbon.

King's chances of making the starting XI did not look good. Even though Rio Ferdinand had been ruled out of the tournament through injury, Eriksson was stilled blessed with enviable strength in depth at centre-half and he had made no secret of the fact that Sol Campbell and John Terry were his first-choice central defensive pairing.

As the game drew closer, Terry picked up a hamstring injury in training. It was not serious enough to warrant drafting in another defender into the squad, but his involvement against France was now in serious doubt. Liverpool's Jamie Carragher was a possible replacement but Eriksson showed his hand in training on the eve of the match when he paired Ledley with Campbell.

'Jamie Carragher is more experienced with international football, but Ledley King is maybe a little bit quicker and a better header,' Eriksson explained. 'You can't give someone experience, the only way is to play them. I'm not worried about it, though, as he seems to be very calm. I don't think he's a nervous person. You can never be sure when you meet Thierry Henry, of course, but I think – and hope – that we are ready. We must keep our shape, though. If you don't have that, you must go home – especially against France. If they find space, they will kill us on the counter-attack.'

Typically, the Spurs man refused to get carried away about his coach's praise or the prospects of playing in what would be the biggest game of his life. 'At the moment, I'm just waiting, but if I do get the chance, I won't let anyone down,' he said. 'I have to train as if I'm going to play. Obviously, we all hope JT [Terry] will be fit, but if anything happens and you're called upon, you have to be focused and you have to be ready. I'm always nervous before a game. I thrive on my nerves, I think I need them to produce my best stuff.'

If he did play, Ledley would be charged with shackling Thierry Henry. The Arsenal striker had scored just once in the seven north London derbies in which the two players had crossed swords, but Ledley was quick to acknowledge the threat the French forward posed to England's Euro 2004 hopes. 'It is not just his pace and skill that set Thierry apart, he's also a big lad with great strength,' he said. 'But I haven't done too bad when I've played against them, although we have not been able to stop Arsenal too many times. How I will try to stop Henry is not something I will talk about publicly. I will talk about it with the team and the coaches. Sven-Göran Eriksson has shown great faith by putting me in the squad, so I'm determined not to let him down.'

One man who was convinced Ledley would not let his country down was Spurs first-team coach Chris Hughton, who had seen him graduate through the club ranks and had no worries about the player being suddenly thrust into the spotlight. 'One thing I'm absolutely positive about is, if he plays, he won't be fazed by it,' Hughton told the

Spurs website. 'That's the type of individual he is. I'll be absolutely delighted if he does play as I'm sure everyone involved with the club will be. He's certainly capable and it's will be up to him to go out and show it. I can see Ledley playing out of his skin and doing well. He is one of those players who you would see as a good international.'

In the end, Terry failed a late fitness test on his hamstring and it was Ledley who ran out at the Estadio Da Luz with the rest of the England team to face France. It was only his sixth cap and his first competitive start for his country, but he was poised to prove that he was more than ready for the challenge.

The atmosphere inside the stadium was electric and France's fluid passing gave them the edge in the early exchanges. Ledley and Campbell were the busier of the centre-half pairings as they fought to keep out Henry and the equally speedy David Trezeguet and it was the latter who had the first genuine chance, but headed over from Patrick Vieira's inviting cross.

England hit back after good interplay between Wayne Rooney and Paul Scholes sent Michael Owen through on goal, but a perfectly timed challenge from William Gallas prevented him from getting his shot away. Ledley was doing a superb job subduing the largely anonymous Henry and England grew in confidence as the first half wore on.

The first goal came seven minutes before the break. French full-back Bixente Lizarazu conceded a free-kick on the right side of his area after fouling David Beckham. The England captain picked himself up and delivered a curling ball into the area; the French defence were unable to clear the danger and Frank Lampard got his head to it first to send the ball past Fabien Barthez.

England held on to their lead going into half-time and the onus was on France to come out in the second 45 minutes to try and manufacture an equaliser. With Ledley and Campbell in imperious form in the heart of the defence, it would not be an easy task.

In truth, France did not look like finding a way of finding a way through the England back four and Eriksson's side should have been out of sight when the impressive Rooney was hacked down by Mikael Silvestre and the referee pointed to the penalty spot. Beckham stepped up to take it but his shot was saved by Barthez and France were still in the game.

That missed opportunity was to prove extremely costly. England seemed to have the points safely in the bag as the match went into injury time, but then substitute Emile Heskey needlessly fouled Henry on the edge of the box. Zinedine Zidane ominously strode forward to take the resulting free-kick and his curling effort gave David James no chance in the England goal. France had conjured up a last-gasp leveller.

There was still time for more drama and, from England's perspective, heartbreak. Eriksson's team were still in a state of shock after the equaliser when Steven Gerrard attempted a risky back pass to James and watched helplessly in horror as Henry set off in pursuit. James came rushing out but, rather than snuffing out the danger, he only managed to haul down the striker and concede a penalty. It was Zidane again who took responsibility and stroked home the spot-kick to hand France an unlikely victory.

England had imploded in injury time with the match at their mercy. It was a disastrous start to the tournament and the British media were quick to sum up the feeling of the team and the fans the day after the match. 'AGONY FOR ENGLAND' ran the *Daily Mail*'s backpage headline while the *Guardian* report ran with the heading of 'DOWN AND OUT IN LISBON'.

The sense of disbelief and disappointment inside the England camp was tangible, but even in the dark days after the game, people inside and outside the squad were talking about Ledley's performance. The Spurs defender had been faultless for England and nullified the threat of Henry with consumate ease. 'Ledley King was absolutely fantastic, not nervous at all. He couldn't have done better,' Eriksson said. 'We thought we had the game won and we should have won it. You can never control France because they have so many attacking options, but in the 90 minutes they did not have many goal-scoring chances. We must be proud, it's tough to lose – we did not deserve to lose.

'If we had lost 3–0 and not created a chance, it would be different. The players are professional. They know they did an excellent job tonight. They did everything we asked of them and, hopefully, it will not be too difficult to lift them up.

'We have to win two games against Switzerland and Croatia and I think we can do that. We played extremely well against the world's best football team. Let's hope we can play France in the Final. We can't always have bad luck.'

England now simply had to win their next two group games to ensure their progress to the quarter-finals and Eriksson had a selection dilemma. John Terry had recovered from his hamstring injury and was fit to face the Swiss in Coimbra and the coach had to decide whether to recall the Chelsea defender or to keep faith with Ledley.

There was growing support for the young Spurs man to keep his place, not least from his club captain Jamie Redknapp, who was in Portugal covering the tournament for the BBC.

'Ledley was different class,' Redknapp said. 'People were questioning him before the game, not because of his ability, but because he hadn't played at the back for most of last season. Even before the game, I was doing a bit of TV and everyone was asking me how he would get on because I know him well from Tottenham. He held Henry no problems, made tackles, made blocks and it was a massive achievement for him. He was excellent and I think he's got to play against Switzerland now.'

Eriksson, however, had different ideas. The Swede had gone into the tournament with Terry and Campbell as his preferred central-defensive pairing and, in the end, he reverted to 'Plan A' and named Terry in the team to face Switzerland. It was a body blow to Ledley after his heroics against the French and he was forced to watch the game from the bench.

The game, at least, went according to plan and England

cantered to a 3–0 victory courtesy of a brace from Wayne Rooney and a third from Steven Gerrard late on. England's challenge was back on track and it was little surprise when Eriksson announced an unchanged side for the final group game against Croatia in Lisbon.

This time, England did not have things all their own way and the alarm bells began ringing when Nico Kovac gave the Croats the lead in the sixth minute after an unseemly goalmouth scramble. England were looking distinctly nervous as they faced the prospect of failing to make the knockout stages of the tournament.

It was not until five minutes before the break that England were back on terms. Michael Owen found space and, although he was denied by the Croatian 'keeper, the ball broke to Rooney. His header flashed invitingly across the face of the goal and Paul Scholes was on hand to steer it into the net. England's second goal came seconds before the half-time whistle when Scholes returned the favour with a delightful flick and Rooney nearly burst the net with his fierce shot. England's nerves were beginning to evaporate.

The second-half ebbed and flowed but England took control of proceedings just past the hour mark. Owen was the creator this time, sending Rooney clean through, and the precocious Everton teenager calmly beat the 'keeper for his second of the match and fourth of the tournament.

It was now time for Eriksson to look to his bench and ensure England did not throw away their priceless lead and the first player he turned to was Ledley, sending him on for Scholes in a holding midfield role. Croatia were still looking dangerous and the coach wanted the added security of the Spurs star breaking up any forays towards the England goal.

The move was a qualified success. Ledley slotted into the midfield seamlessly but Croatia did pull a goal back with an Igor Tudor header on 74 minutes. The game was once again in the balance, albeit briefly, and Eriksson was indebted to Frank Lampard who drilled home England's fourth five minutes later to seal the win and the team's place in the quarter-finals.

'If we play as we did in the first half it will not be easy to beat us,' a relieved Eriksson said after the final whistle. 'We deserved to win today and I'm very proud of the players. It is now important that we try to recover as quickly as possible and as intelligently as possible. We played very good football in the first half and controlled everything. It was a pity they scored a second.'

For Ledley, it was his seventh cap and, although he had played 20 minutes in midfield rather than central defence, he was still very much in the manager's thoughts and in contention for a place in the side to face Portugal in the last eight. The tournament, it seemed, would yet see more of the 23-year-old in action.

On the day of the Portugal game, however, Ledley found himself on a plane back to England rather than out on the pitch against the hosts. Fate had conspired to end his tournament without him kicking another ball in anger. When he'd joined the squad, Ledley had left his pregnant girlfriend Stephanie Carter at home. The baby wasn't due until late August, but while the rest of the players were focusing on the quarter-finals, Ledley was being told that she had gone into labour. A frantic dash ensued as he raced back to be at the birth and all thoughts of football, Euro 2004 and England were forgotten.

'We were not allowed to have our phones on at the team hotel, so the FA got a call from my girlfriend on the day of the Portugal game,' Ledley explained in an interview with the *Sun* after the dramatic events. 'She had gone into labour. At first, it was not too much of a shock when I was told. There was always a chance [my son] Coby was going to be premature. She had already been in hospital due to a few problems. Even so, I was not expecting him to be born while I was in Portugal.

'I spoke to Sven Göran Eriksson and he said, "There are bigger things than football." He said it was totally up to me. I had a strong feeling I was going to be on the bench anyway. I was gutted I was going to miss the match. I was told at 9.30 on the morning of the match – I was still in bed at the time.

'The FA were really good. I was on a flight at noon, got to London and the FA put on a car for me to go around the M25 and get to Chelmsford. I got to the hospital at 4.00pm. Being on the plane was a funny situation. I didn't want to leave Euro 2004 early. I was leaving Portugal and all my team-mates were still there. It was strange being on the plane on my own. But apart from that disappointment, it was overshadowed by the birth.

'After landing, although still on the plane, I switched on my phone. Immediately, my girlfriend rang to tell me she'd had the baby about 15 minutes earlier. Initially, I was disappointed as I wanted to be there. But then I just wanted to get there as soon as possible and make sure they were both OK. He was due on 23 or 24 August, and ended up being born on 24 June.'

Ledley's joy was in stark contrast to the emotions of the England players he had left behind. The quarter-final against Portugal was an epic encounter with countless twists and turns. Eriksson's side took the lead after just three minutes through Michael Owen. Portugal equalised courtesy of Ledley's Tottenham team-mate Helder Postiga and the clash went into extra-time. The hosts edged in front with a goal from Rui Costa but England drew level five minutes later courtesy of Frank Lampard. The two teams could not be separated after 120 minutes and the game went to a penalty shootout. England fans prayed the team's shootout jinx would not strike again but their prayers went unanswered and Portugal triumphed 6–5 to send Eriksson and his team home.

Ledley had to endure the drama in front of a television. An England win would have presented him with the dilemma of whether to stay in England with Stephanie and Coby or return to Portugal, but the penalty shootout made the decision for him.

'Sitting at home watching England go out of Euro 2004 on penalties was terrible,' he admitted. 'But having a son born nine weeks premature on the very same day put things into perspective. Sometimes, there are tougher things than losing on penalties.'

His season was over. The new campaign was just around the corner but, for the time being, he could focus on his new baby. It was also time to reflect. His involvement at Euro 2004 had been limited to 90 superb minutes against France and a 20-minute cameo in the Croatia game, but no one was now in any doubt of his international credentials.

'Euro 2004 will definitely have helped me confidence-wise,' he said. 'I have always believed in my ability but, sometimes at international level, you need an opportunity. This was my opportunity, even though it was in unfortunate circumstances due to John Terry's injury.' Ledley added that he felt that he could only have done his cause some good, although he was well aware of the competition for places in the current England set-up. To become a first-choice central defender would be a tough ask. He also admitted that he'd been surprised at playing in midfield for England, and that he hadn't been relishing the thought. But having done a job there, and having received a great deal of credit, he hoped that it would now go some way to confirming in Eriksson's mind – and the mind of the public and media – that international football is where he now belonged. Time and fate permitting, Ledley would discover soon enough whether his hopes of becoming a regular in the England side would be realised.

6

KING OF THE LANE

When Tottenham reported back for pre-season training in the summer of 2004, there was a sense of renewed optimism spreading throughout the club. The disappointments of the previous campaign had been consigned to history and, with a new manager, a radical overhaul of the coaching set-up and money to spend in the transfer market, the atmosphere was unashamedly upbeat.

Jacques Santini arrived at White Hart Lane just two weeks after the end of the European Championships and, after the prolonged uncertainty of David Pleat's caretaker reign, the players and the fans now had a permanent coach with a glittering CV and a hard-earned reputation as one of the best managers in Europe. He was the kind of high-profile appointment the supporters had been baying for and the club seemed ready finally to shake off their mid-table mediocrity and start pushing for a top-six finish.

'I'm ready,' Santini confidently announced when he was officially unveiled. 'I am ready for my new club. I am very happy. I have looked at the stadium and it is magnificent. I am looking forward to my first season at Tottenham. The chance to coach here and in the Premiership is very, very beautiful for me. We have five weeks to prepare for the season. We have confidence in the players and it is very important to begin the season with two or three good results. This is the first objective for the new season.'

Santini, however, was not the only new face to be seen at the training ground. Spurs had decided to adopt a Continental coaching set-up and that meant bringing in Dane Frank Arnesen as the club's Sporting Director, as well as highly-rated Frenchman Dominique Cuperly and Dutchman Martin Jol as assistant coaches. It was a radical and ambitious overhaul of the system – although Chris Hughton was to remain on the staff – but after too many seasons of underachievement, it was clear the Tottenham board felt it was time for a change.

Arnesen arrived from Dutch side PSV Eindhoven, where had spent a decade as the club's director of football. A former Danish international, his remit was signing new players and the club's scouting programme and he was quick to acknowledge the size of the task ahead him when he faced the British media for the first time.

'It's a big challenge but that's why we do it,' he conceded. 'All sportsmen have a big ambition level and I'm the same. I think I'm joining probably the best league in the world... the challenge is big and the competition here between the clubs is enormously hard. That is the challenge and I look forward to it.

'I'm delighted and happy to be here, finally. It was a bit of a strange time the last couple of weeks because I was still working for PSV but I'm here now alongside Jacques, Martin Jol and we can now get things started for next season. It was a big decision. I've been at PSV for 19 years, so it was always going to be difficult. I was there as a player and the last ten years as sporting director. It was difficult to leave but I took a big decision and the chance at a big club in London – Tottenham Hotspur – came along. So on one hand it's sad but on the other, I'm hoping to do a very good job here.'

Jol was a familiar face to some in England after stints as a player with West Bromwich Albion and Coventry in the 1980s. He had been forging a growing reputation as a manager in Holland with RKC Waalwijk but insisted he had no reservations about accepting the role of assistant coach to Santini.

'It wasn't a hard decision for me to come,' he said. 'If many other clubs had asked me to become assistant to the head coach I wouldn't have done it, having managed and trained in Holland for 15 years. Spurs is different. I had a two-or three-minute talk with my wife and we said we have to do it.

'I was six years at my old club and it was a big

challenge. I knew Frank Arnesen – not personally – from PSV Eindhoven and he knew me. He and Jacques Santini have shown a lot of confidence in me and the Premiership is where I wanted to go. It was an easy decision.

'I have already met some people and it is just like all those years ago when I played in England – still the same atmosphere and nice pitches. I am looking forward to starting the job properly.'

With the new-look coaching set-up in place, it was time for Santini and his lieutenants to assess the squad. The first phase was a training camp in Sweden but Ledley was given extra time off to recover from his Euro 2004 exertions and did not travel. In truth, Santini did not need to run the rule over the 23-year-old after seeing his imperious performance for England against France over the summer. The former French manager had witnessed first-hand the way he had handled Thierry Henry in Lisbon and there was no doubt in his mind that Ledley was the player around whom the rest of the team could be built.

Inevitably, however, there were changes to the squad as the summer wore on. Gus Poyet, Christian Ziege, Stephen Carr, Gary Doherty, Darren Anderton, Helder Postiga and Sergei Rebrov were all moved out as Santini set about moulding a squad in his image and, with Arnesen's help, Leeds goalkeeper Paul Robinson, Fulham midfielder Sean Davis, Porto playmaker Pedro Mendes, West Ham duo Michael Carrick and Jermain Defoe and Coventry defender Calum Davenport were all brought in.

Spurs had again spent big in an effort to revitalise the

team but what was immediately clear was that the club was now targeting younger talent in a conscious rejection of the previous policy of signing experienced players. The exception to the rule was the move for veteran Moroccan central defender Noureddine Naybet from Spanish side Deportivo La Coruña but, overall, Tottenham were now focusing on youth. Even at the age of 23, Ledley was fast becoming one of the side's elder statesmen.

Ledley returned for the club's domestic pre-season games against Hull City, Sheffield United and Nottingham Forest and, once the team had competed in the Kappa Cup in Seville, they were almost ready for the new season. A game with Serie A outfit Cagliari at the Lane and a visit to Glasgow to play Celtic were last-minute opportunities for Santini to fine-tune his side before it was time for the real action.

Liverpool were the visitors to White Hart Lane for the season's opener and Ledley was paired with Naybet in central defence in a side with five new signings in the ranks. The Reds would be a severe examination of Santini's new-look team.

The visitors dominated for large chunks of the match but Spurs refused to buckle under the pressure. Liverpool took a first-half lead through French striker Djibril Cissé but Tottenham showed a resilience that had been too often lacking the previous season and earned a share of the points when Jermain Defoe scored his first for the club with 20 minutes left. It had not been a great performance but there were positives on which to build and the young players had acquitted themselves well.

'I thought it came together pretty well against Liverpool, especially with so many players making their débuts,' Ledley told the Spurs website after the game. 'We've had to gel quickly and find our way of playing with the new manager and staff.

'We've got a young squad and I'm one of the most experienced players in there. I've got to help the younger ones as some of the older players helped me when I was coming through. I have to use my experience on the pitch to help them. I still class myself as quite a young player but, with the squad here, I have to step up and be more of a leader.'

One particularly interested observer in the White Hart Lane crowd was Sven-Göran Eriksson. Later that day, the England manager was to announce his squad for the friendly against Ukraine in Newcastle and, after witnessing another assured performance from Ledley against Liverpool, he had no hesitation in naming him in his starting line-up alongside Chelsea's John Terry.

A crowd of over 35,000 descended on St James' Park to watch England's first game of the new season and they were not disappointed by what they saw. England seemed to have shaken off the bitter disappointment of their penalty shoot-out misery against Portugal and produced a vibrant, attacking display that boded well for their forthcoming World Cup qualifiers in September.

The first goal of the night owed much to a large slice of luck when Terry mis-hit a cross after 27 minutes and the ball fell fortuitously at David Beckham's feet for a simple tap in. It was early in the second-half when

Michael Owen headed home a second from Beckham's cross from eight yards out and substitute Shaun Wright-Phillips, on his début, rounded off a perfect night for England with a dazzling solo run from inside his own half that he finished in convincing style. England looked in fine fettle.

'I always expect England to play good football and perform well and they did that,' Eriksson said after the game. 'It was a very good match and we played very well. All 17 players made a contribution. I'm happy for the players, for me and for the fans.'

Although it was the three goals that gave the supporters cause to cheer, Ledley's performance at the back did not go unnoticed and his commanding, athletic display was evidence that his outstanding 90 minutes against France in the summer was far from a flash in the pan. 'It was another important match for King,' reflected the BBC Sport website, 'getting in more valuable international experience which he will need as England look ahead to games against Austria and Poland in September. He looked assured at the back and was comfortable playing against Andriy Shevchenko, one of the best strikers in European football.' The *Daily Mirror* was equally impressed: 'He hardly missed a tackle all night but was left exposed early on by the midfield not doing their job. He had his work cut out with so many Ukraine bodies surging forward.'

The praise was not limited to the media; Ledley's England team-mates were also quick to pay tribute to his growing maturity and influence on the side. 'Ledley is so calm under pressure and makes the right decisions,' Terry, his old Senrab team-mate, said. 'When he needs to be cool, he is, and when it's necessary to get stuck in, he does that, too. For me, he has all the makings of a true quality defender.'

Ledley returned to White Hart Lane brimming with confidence and Spurs were to enjoy the dividends as the team embarked on a three-match unbeaten run that suggested Santini had finally found some of the answers to the team's perennial problems. Newcastle were beaten 1–0 at St James's Park thanks to a goal from Cameroon defender Thimothée Atouba and, although the side were held to a 1–1 draw by West Brom at the Hawthorns four days later, Spurs were making genuine progress.

The Hawthorns clash wasn't a classic but it was nonetheless another watershed in Ledley's career. The match was 78 minutes old when Santini felt he needed fresh legs on the pitch and he decided to sacrifice club captain Jamie Redknapp in favour of the more dynamic Michael Brown. Redknapp began to make his way to the touchline but, before he left the field, he handed the captain's armband to Ledley. The 23-year-old was now the team's leader.

Santini decided to rest Redknapp for the following game – the visit of Birmingham to the Lane – and Ledley was named as captain from the start. It was a big honour for such a relatively young player but the Spurs supporters loved it because he had come through the ranks at the club and his elevation reflected Santini's faith in him. The fact that Tottenham marked the occasion with a 1–0 victory to make it two wins and two draws in their opening four league fixtures was the icing on the cake.

'I am pleased with our fighting spirit because when it was difficult, we stuck together,' Santini said after the match. 'That was very important. Birmingham are a good team with good players. I thought Jesper Gronkjaer was a threat down the right and their strikers were very impressive. I know my team is tired but we played together. We have a young team with new players and to have that fighting spirit is good news for the future.'

The day after the game, Eriksson announced his squad for the two World Cup qualifiers away to Austria and Poland. In previous seasons, Ledley had waited with bated breath to see if he had been selected but this time he knew his inclusion was a foregone conclusion. His natural modesty would never have allowed him to admit it, but the truth was that he was now an integral part of the England set-up and with his injury problems were a thing of the past; Eriksson could rely on the Spurs man to anchor his defence.

The international break gave Ledley a chance to reflect on what had been a whirlwind first month of the new season. Spurs had made a hugely encouraging start to the campaign, he had excelled for England against Ukraine and he had now captained his club. It was almost more than he could have wished for.

'I'm a young player but I'm probably the most experienced player at Tottenham in terms of playing for Spurs,' he told the Football Association website in the build-up to the Austria game in Vienna. 'That comes with a bit of responsibility and I've been given the captain's armband on a couple of occasions this season. That has helped, too, and has probably taken my game on a little bit more funnily enough.

'I don't think I'm a shouting captain; hopefully, I lead by example. But you have to give orders on the pitch as a defender and communicate with the team. I don't give too many players rollockings at the moment but maybe that will come. I don't think I've changed too much, but maybe I'll get more vocal the more experienced I get.

'Mr Santini has been very good with me. He's a manager of great experience and giving me responsibility has helped as well. He's asked for my opinion in certain situations and that's great for a young guy. We have a good understanding and it bodes well for the future.'

Ledley looked certain to start against Austria with Terry in central defence but, with Sol Campbell and Jonathan Woodgate nearing full fitness and Rio Ferdinand poised to return after his nine-month ban for missing a mandatory drugs test, he knew the competition for England places was going to intensify in the very near future.

'We have some great defenders in this country but if you do get your chance you can only go in there and try to do your best,' he said. 'Hopefully, if I get the chance, I can show the manager I'm worthy of playing and that he can count on me in the future.'

Ledley did indeed line up in England's starting XI in the Ernst Happel Stadium in Vienna to face the Austrians.

More than 45,000 fans had packed the stadium to create an intimidating atmosphere for the visitors but Eriksson's side seemed to relish their surroundings and began the match the better of the two teams.

The first goal came on 23 minutes. England were awarded a free-kick inside the area by the Slovakian referee after Austrian keeper Alex Manninger was deemed to have handled a back pass. David Beckham stood over the dead ball but, rather than blast it as the defence clearly expected him to, he found Frank Lampard, who couldn't miss from close range. England were the dominant side and they had the lead they deserved.

They should have doubled their advantage soon after the break when Michael Owen manufactured space for Alan Smith just eight yards out, but Manninger atoned for his earlier aberration with an excellent, one-handed reflex save. A second England goal was coming and it was Steven Gerrard who provided it just past the hour with a elegantly struck, long-range effort that flew into the top corner. The visitors were in complete control and Ledley had never had a more comfortable 60 minutes of international football.

Roared on by their vociferous fans, Austria rallied and gave themselves hope with 20 minutes left when Roland Kollmann stroked home a superb free-kick. England were still in the ascendancy but the home side had given themselves a lifeline, and just two minutes later they were on terms. It had been Manninger who was culpable in the build-up to England's first goal, but his mistake paled into insignificance compared to David James' howler at the other end. Andreas Ivanschitz struck a speculative drive from outside the area, James seemed to have the effort in his sights but, at the crucial moment, he inexplicably dived over the ball and watched ashen-faced as it crept into the net.

Eriksson threw Jermain Defoe into the fray in a desperate attempt to repair the damage. The Spurs striker hit a post before the final whistle but it was too little too late and the match ended in a 2–2 draw. England had squandered a two-goal lead and the celebrations of the Austrian players at the final whistle left little doubt which side was happier with a share of the spoils.

'It was disappointing to see the free-kick go in and disappointing to see their second goal go in,' Eriksson admitted in his post-match press conference. 'I am disappointed because I thought we played well enough to win the game. After going 2–0 ahead, we created golden opportunities to finish the game, but didn't. I'm sure we were good enough to win. We did well in the first half and had complete control. They pushed some players up in the second half but I don't think they created any good chances at all.

'We should have made it 3–0 and, with 20 minutes to go, it looked like we should win the game. We have to keep our heads up and go to Poland to win the game. Poland have won today so that makes it even more important for us to get the victory there on Wednesday.

'I hope we play like we did in the first half against Austria for the whole game. To be top of the group, we have to win the game. If we do that, it won't be bad for us to have four points after two games. There were a lot of positives to take from the Austria game. Things happen in football, but I am feeling really positive. We have not won games we should have lately and it has happened too many times. I hope and I think we can learn from it.'

England made the short trip to Poland for the game in Chorzow with stinging media criticism of their performance in Vienna ringing in their ears and the need for a morale-boosting win was paramount. Ledley and Terry escaped the barrage of negative coverage and kept their places in the side as Eriksson looked to get the qualifying campaign back on track.

As they had done in Austria at the weekend, England started the stronger of the two sides and Defoe was presented with the first decent chance after Wayne Bridge and Ashley Cole combined well, but the Tottenham forward blazed his volley wide. Eriksson had brought Defoe into the starting line-up in place of Manchester United's Alan Smith and Ledley's club mate made amends for his earlier miss nine minutes before half-time with a defence-splitting turn and fizzing shot that flew past Polish 'keeper Jerzy Dudek.

The lead lasted for just two minutes of the second period. Poland broke upfield, Kamil Kosowski played in Maciej Zurawski and he gave Paul Robinson no chance with a powerful finish. England were staring down the barrel and failure to secure all three points would only intensify the pressure on Eriksson and his players.

Luck had not been on their side in Vienna four days

before when James gifted the Austrians a goal, but the roles were reversed in Poland as the home side contrived to put the ball into their own net. Cole surged down the left and delivered an inviting cross into the box which Polish defender Arkadiusz Glowacki only succeeded in steering past Dudek. Fortune had smiled on the visitors and now they had to keep Poland out for the final 32 minutes. The Polish onslaught failed to materialise, however, and it was England who went closest to a third goal through Bridge and then Michael Owen, with England eventually holding on for a 2–1 win.

Only two games of the qualification campaign had been played, but the sense of relief was obvious. The press had turned on Eriksson alarmingly quickly after the Austrian misadventure and, with England facing two further qualifying matches against Wales and Azerbaijan in October, it was crucial the players reported back for club duty with a victory and restored sense of calm.

Ledley had again looked to the manor born but, for once, it was two other Spurs players whom Eriksson chose to single out for particular praise after the match. 'I think we played mainly very well,' Eriksson enthused in his press conference. 'The performance we did today was as good as Saturday, but this time we got the victory. We played very well for the 90 minutes. Today it is congratulations to the team, they all did very, very well. Both Defoe and Robinson played very, very well. Jermain was the goalscorer. He is a huge talent, quick and a great scorer and I am very happy for him. Robinson did everything that he should do, but did it very calmly. We battled here, but we were a little bit sloppy and not aggressive enough for some of the time in Austria, and you can't afford to do that at international level.

'I'm sorry to say the media over-reacted after we drew in Austria. People were saying the World Cup dream was over after one game and one draw. It is very difficult to understand. After Saturday's performance, we were criticised as individuals and as a team. Whether that was fair or not fair is up to other people to say. But the only thing you can do against criticism is to play good football and to win.'

Bolstered by the result, the Spurs trio returned to White Hart Lane in high spirits and there was much to be optimistic about at club level as well. Tottenham were unbeaten in the league, the club had three players in the England starting line-up and, in Santini, the board finally seemed to have found exactly the right man for the job.

Ledley was particularly pleased with the team's far more convincing displays at the back after some alarmingly porous performances the previous season, but admitted even he was surprised at just how quickly the new players had gelled with the existing squad. 'We are all pulling together and the team spirit is really good,' he said in an interview with the club website. 'It is fair to say we've looked a lot more steady this season, with two clean sheets and that is a great start. Hopefully, we can pick it up again after the little break and carry on. There have been a lot of new players and I don't think we expected it to click into place as soon as it has. The lads have dug deep and shown a great team spirit already.'

The next test of the side's resolve was newly-promoted Norwich at the Lane. Jamie Redknapp returned to reclaim the captain's armband and the home fans expected a barrage of goals after the Canaries had leaked nine in their opening four Premiership outings. Spurs applied all the early pressure but the visitors were being surprisingly stubborn at the back and their best chance came midway through the first half when Defoe struck a fierce volley from outside the area that was cleared off the line. Defoe struck a post after the break but the match seemed to be drifting to a disappointing draw until the last 15 minutes when Norwich launched a rare foray into the final third. Darren Huckerby found space, clipped the ball over Paul Robinson and the crowd waited in collective horror for the striker to roll the ball into the Tottenham net. They – and Huckerby – hadn't reckoned on Ledley, however, who seemed to appear from nowhere, slide in behind the striker and hook the ball to safety. Ledley's intervention was immediately a contender for tackle of the season but, more importantly, it preserved the team's unbeaten record and ensured a second clean sheet.

After the match, Santini admitted he was disappointed not to have taken all three points but acknowledged that Ledley's tackle was a pivotal point in the game. 'It is possibly two points dropped,' he said, 'but when Huckerby went around Paul Robinson, it was possible for Norwich to score and therefore for us to lose the game. At the end of the championship, we might see it as a point won, but I am a little disappointed because the effort of my players wasn't compensated. My team had a good game. We have seven or eight good chances to score but [Norwich 'keeper] Green was the Man of the Match.'

A third consecutive clean sheet was just around the corner. Tottenham travelled to Stamford Bridge to face Chelsea, who were now managed by the highly rated Portuguese coach José Mourinho, and Santini knew this was the biggest challenge for his side to date. They were to handle it with aplomb. Ledley again partnered Noureddine Naybet in the heart of the defence and the gnarled African veteran and young Englishman combined to such good effect that Chelsea had only one real chance in the game – an Eidur Gudjohnsen shot that hit the post. It wasn't the prettiest performance in Tottenham's history but it was undeniably effective.

Mourinho was hugely critical of the Spurs approach in his post-match press conference but his comments must have been music to Ledley's ears. 'As we say in Portugal, they brought the bus and they left the bus in front of the goal,' Mourinho moaned. 'I would have been frustrated if I had been a supporter who paid £50 to watch this game because Spurs came to defend. I'm really frustrated because there was only one team looking to win, they only came not to concede – it's not fair for the football we played.'

A 6–0 drubbing of Oldham in the second round of the League Cup got the side back to goal-scoring ways and they then awaited the challenge of Manchester United at White Hart Lane with a quiet confidence. It was a tight game from the start and it took a penalty, ultimately, to separate the two sides – Erik Edman tugged back John O'Shea in the area and Ruud van Nistelrooy converted the resulting spot-kick late in the first half. Spurs had surrendered their unbeaten start to the league season but the nature of their defeat against United still boded well for the rest of the campaign.

It was time for Sven-Göran Eriksson to reveal his latest England squad for the qualifiers against Wales and Azerbaijan. Rio Ferdinand had completed his suspension and Sol Campbell was fit again and the Swede didn't hesitate in bringing both players back immediately. Ledley and John Terry now had a real fight on their hands.

Eriksson acknowledged he was delighted to have Ferdinand and Campbell available for selection once again, but was also at pains to point out they wouldn't necessarily walk back into the starting line-up. 'Having two such players back would be good news for any manager – but with Ledley King and John Terry having proved such able deputies, it only adds to the selection headache,' Eriksson said. 'It gives me a problem but it is an extremely good problem to have. If you talk about Campbell and Ferdinand at the World Cup in Japan, they were the best central defenders in the whole tournament and I think I'm not the only one saying that. What I can see with Rio now is that he's very hungry for football and Manchester United are very happy to have him back. He's a leader, he was the captain on Tuesday for his club which was nice to see, and he gives calm to the back line.

'But also we have Ledley King and John Terry playing extremely maturely and very well for England. I think we have four very good central defenders now. It's almost a luxury to have four centre-halves like that, but we have it. Who is going to play? Well, I have ideas but the training will decide that. And whatever I choose, it's a good choice.'

Ledley joined up with the rest of the squad for the Wales game at Old Trafford acutely aware that his place in the team was under threat. He had never let his country down in ten previous appearances but, as the days before the big match came and went, the writing seemed on the wall and the 23-year-old looked destined for a place on the bench. Eriksson was yet to confirm his team officially, but Ledley was already in philosophical mood about his probable omission. 'Me and John Terry have played the last couple of games and I think we've done pretty well,' he said in a pre-match interview with the Football Association website. 'But we know Rio and Sol are first choice and are likely to come in. It's quite difficult to take, but that's football. We haven't been told anything yet but, at the end of the day, we know they are the first choice. We just have to take the decision and train as hard as possible. Everybody is 100 per cent focused with England and it's really good for the country that we have so many good players coming through in defence, even if it makes it tough for me.

'In the end, we're a team and you need all your players together. We win as a team and we lose as a team. So whoever is not playing on Saturday will support those who are. That's what I'll be doing if I'm not playing... nobody will be sat on the bench sulking, I can promise that.

'I'll be ready if I play and ready if I don't. It's great for my confidence that I'm still in the squad with so many big-name players available again. I still think things are going well for me this season because Tottenham have got off to a good start and I've had more responsibility there and I'm enjoying it. Last season was difficult, playing out of position in midfield at times, but I'm back where I want to play and I have to show I'm good enough to start for England. That's my challenge.

'It's tough to be left out, if I am, but the country should be happy we have got so many good players in that position. Rio has come back in and he's been class in training. It looks like he's never been away and he's a great player, no one can argue with that.'

Eriksson certainly couldn't and, as predicted, he recalled both Ferdinand and Campbell to face the Welsh. Ledley and Terry would keep each other company on the bench.

The match was, at least, a happy one from an England perspective; they scored with their first attack of the game through Frank Lampard and made it a comfortable win 15 minutes from time courtesy of a trademark David Beckham free-kick. Ledley came on for the final four minutes in place of Wayne Rooney but the game was over as a contest and his involvement was superfluous.

England did not have long to dwell on their victory as they headed east to the Azerbaijan capital of Baku for their second qualifier in five days. Ledley celebrated his 24th birthday the day before the game, but Eriksson was in no mood to give him a belated present and once again opted for Ferdinand and Campbell as his central defenders. This time, there was to be no cameo appearance for the Spurs defender as England ground out a 1–0 win and he headed back to north London with a mere four minutes of football to his name for his troubles.

Unsurprisingly, he kept his frustration to himself on his return to club duty and received a timely boost just days later when it was announced he had been named the Barclays Player of the Month for September. He was the first defender to collect the award since Rio Ferdinand in October 2001 and it was fitting recognition of his growing maturity in the heart of the Tottenham defence.

'Ledley King has returned to club football in fantastic form after playing a key role in England's Euro 2004 campaign,' said the awards panel's Nic Gault. 'His defensive performance against Chelsea at Stamford Bridge was first-class, rightly earning him the Barclays Man of the Match Award. King was instrumental in Tottenham's strong defensive record throughout September… it's not surprising team-mates and pundits alike single him out for praise.'

Unfortunately, the award was to prove a millstone around Ledley and Spurs' neck and the elation of being acknowledged by his peers quickly turned to agony as Tottenham endured a horrific October. Defeats against Portsmouth, Bolton and Fulham comprehensively put the brakes on what had previously a good start to the Premiership season and, even though Wanderers were seen off in the League Cup, the team suffered an alarming dip in form.

Worse was to follow. October gave way to November but, before the side had the opportunity to rectify things on the pitch, the club were stunned by the news that Jacques Santini was leaving the club. The former France manager had been in charge for just 13 games – losing only four – but now he was suddenly heading back across the Channel. Confusion reigned and a statement from Santini by way of explanation did little to dampen the speculation about his abrupt departure: 'My time at Tottenham has been memorable and it is with deep regret that I take my leave,' the Frenchman said. 'Private issues in my personal life have arisen which caused my decision. I have therefore requested to return to France. I very much hope that the wonderful fans will respect my decision. I should like to thank Frank Arnesen and Daniel Levy for their understanding. I wish the club and the supporters all the best for the season.'

The media sensed a story and, once he was safely back in France, Santini shed a little light on what had really happened behind the scenes at White Hart Lane. 'It was hard from the start at Spurs,' he admitted in an interview with a French TV station. 'There was a problem around where responsibility lay in the club, especially when it came to transfer policy where we could never reach agreement. We never found a way of agreeing how to prepare for the season and how to buy the players.

'Perhaps we could have spoken when I signed my contract to make things clear. I was told I would be in charge of all first-team matters – buying and selling players and doing the coaching. But things were not well defined because, as soon as I arrived, it became clear I was only in charge of coaching.'

Santini had walked out on Friday. Tottenham faced Charlton at the Lane the following day and the club decided to place Martin Jol in temporary charge of the first team. Ledley was set to play for the fifth manager of his professional career.

The sense of confusion that surrounded Santini's exit sadly crept into the performance of the players. Jol had less than 24 hours to work with the team and it showed against Charlton as they looked all at sea and they were three down inside 50 minutes. Robbie Keane and Jermain Defoe gave Tottenham fleeting hope with late goals, but the first game under Jol ended in a 3–2 defeat.

The club was in a state of turmoil on and off the pitch. 'It was a big surprise for us on Friday but we have to go on,' said Jol after the game. 'The first half we saw that it wasn't easy for the players. We didn't do things differently. The only thing we did was play Robbie Keane on the left instead of [Reto] Ziegler, the rest was the same formation. A few players looked tired. I was not happy when I came out because they scored for 3–0 and you really have problems as a coach. It was a nightmare. But after that we showed great character to come back and we could have easily had a draw with some luck.'

The Tottenham players and fans now waited to see what the board would do about the managerial vacuum. Memories of the previous season and David Pleat's extended but ultimately unsuccessful caretaker tenure were still fresh in the memory. No one wanted to witness another period of prolonged uncertainty and the club's board evidently agreed as they announced, just three days after Santini's volte-face, that Jol was the new manager. Spurs had lost one manager and found another in the space of a week.

'These things happen in football and you have to get on with it quickly,' Ledley reflected after Jol's appointment was confirmed. 'Everyone enjoyed working with Martin while Jacques was here and it is nice that he is in charge now. His methods are a little bit different and I think he wants to bring a bit of the old Tottenham football back into it... He is a tough character who is passionate about his football and, hopefully, that will shine through in the team.'

Jol faced a baptism of fire in his game as the new boss – Arsenal at White Hart Lane. Redknapp's absence from the starting line-up saw the Dutchman follow Santini's lead and make Ledley captain and Spurs welcomed their oldest rivals looking for a first league win over the Gunners for five years.

The derby did not disappoint in terms of excitement and drama but there was to be no fairytale victory for Jol. Tottenham initially followed the script when Naybet scored from close range but they fatally allowed Arsenal to equalise seconds before the half-time whistle through Thierry Henry, who scored a rare goal against a Spurs side with his nemesis Ledley in the centre of the defence.

The second period was a dazzling procession of seven goals. Arsenal took the lead with a Lauren penalty ten minutes after the restart after Noé Pamarot was adjudged to have fouled Freddie Ljungberg. Patrick Vieira extended the visitors' lead but Jermain Defoe pulled one back after beating three defenders, before Ljungberg scored Arsenal's fourth. Ledley tried to inspire a fightback when he rose above the Arsenal defence to head home Michael Carrick's free-kick, but Robert Pires put the result beyond doubt and Freddie Kanouté's late strike was merely a consolation. Spurs had lost a nine-goal thriller.

'You can't make errors like we did and win football matches,' a disappointed Jol said after the game. 'I have some good feelings about the game but also some horrible feelings as well. If you score four goals against Arsenal, or any team, at home, you expect to win comfortably. Arsenal are dangerous on the counter-attack but we made big errors. You cannot give the ball away at the back. We have to build on the positive things. We showed everyone we can score goals, but we have to improve our defensive play. We cannot give the ball away and concede goals like we did.'

The Premiership now took a brief break for midweek internationals. England were to play Spain at the Bernabeu in Madrid but the bad news for club and country was that Ledley was forced to pull out of Sven-Göran Eriksson's squad. He had completed the full 90 minutes against Arsenal but his old knee problem had flared up and it was decided not to risk him unnecessarily against the Spanish in what was only a friendly.

'It is a pity to be without Ledley King,' Eriksson admitted as he prepared to take his side to the Spanish capital. 'In defence, we are missing Sol Campbell. His absence would be felt by any team and it is a shame that we miss Ledley King, too.'

Fortunately, the enforced rest worked wonders and the 24-year-old was fit and raring to go as the league swung back into action. Spurs headed to the Midlands to face Aston Villa but came away smarting from a 1–0 defeat that made it six successive Premiership losses. The side's alarming slump was not all of Jol's making, but the affable Dutchman and his players were already under intense pressure and victory against Middlesbrough at White Hart Lane was absolutely essential.

Spurs certainly showed a renewed sense of purpose against 'Boro but it was ultimately a refereeing decision that swung the game. French defender Franck Queudrue badly mistimed an ugly-looking tackle on Pamarot in the 40th minute and referee Phil Dowd deemed the challenge was worthy of a straight red card. Middlesbrough would have to play the whole of the second half with ten men, and Spurs took full advantage of their numerical supremacy. Defoe struck first, just three minutes after the break, converting Pedro Mendes' inviting cross, and Kanouté ensured Tottenham's horrendous run would finally come to an end with the second 15 minutes from time. Jol had his first league win as coach and Spurs could start planning the revival.

A heartbreaking penalty shoot-out loss to Liverpool in the quarter-final of the League Cup was a temporary blip and, as Jol quickly settled into his new job, Tottenham embarked on an impressive run of

Premiership victories. Blackburn, Manchester City, Southampton and Norwich were all dispatched and, although Crystal Palace held Spurs at White Hart Lane, the side were back to winning ways in the next game as Everton were put to the sword in a 5–2 mauling at White Hart Lane on New Year's Day.

The arrival of 2005 saw the transfer window open once again and Spurs were about to indulge in a piece of business that was to have a fundamental impact on Ledley's career. Club captain Jamie Redknapp had been a peripheral figure in the team's recent upturn in fortunes and the 31-year-old had become an almost permanent fixture on the Tottenham bench over the last two months. His father, Harry Redknapp, was managing Southampton and, when the Saints boss made an enquiry about his son, Spurs were willing to let the former England midfielder go to the south coast. The deal was finalised in early January and Redknapp left White Hart Lane.

Jol now needed a new club captain and there was only credible candidate. Ledley had been captaining the side as Redknapp kicked his heels among the substitutes and the Dutch manager had no hesitation in handing his star player the captain's armband on a permanent basis. Even at the age of 24, Ledley was already the longest-serving player at the club and had earned the respect of his team-mates and the supporters alike.

'I've learned a lot from Jamie and we all wish him well at Southampton,' Ledley told the club website after his appointment. 'It is an honour to be captain... we've got a great side with the best team spirit we've had for years. It is a good time to be playing for the club and everyone is enjoying it.

'Of course, I've seen some great captains over the years here and it is amazing for me to be given the chance. Jamie was a great player, captain and ambassador for the club so it is nice to take over from him. I think I've got to be natural and be the way that I am as captain. I think that is what will work best for me, but obviously you learn things from other captains and maybe bring bits into your game slowly. I think it is best to be natural, though. I don't think much has changed too much in my head. I've had the armband for a few games and you feel great when you are wearing it.'

The first test of Ledley's leadership came at Old Trafford. Manchester United were unbeaten at home all season and had won eight of their previous nine league games while Spurs had not won at the home of the Red Devils for 16 long years. With United desperate to make up ground on the leaders Chelsea, it was going to be a difficult 90 minutes.

Predictably, United enjoyed the lion's share of possession on their own ground but a succession of fine saves from Paul Robinson and dogged defending from Ledley and the rest of the Spurs back four held them at bay. A goalless draw seemed the likely outcome and, had it not been for one of the most controversial refereeing decisions in the history of the Premiership, Tottenham would have had come away with a famous victory.

As the second-half neared its end, Spurs made a rare

foray into the opposition half and United 'keeper Roy Carroll rushed out of his area to make a clearance. The ball fell to Pedro Mendes, a full 60 yards out and, as Carroll scrambled back into his area, the Portuguese midfielder launched a wildly ambitious, looping shot towards the United goal. Carroll managed to get back on his line just as Mendes' effort zeroed in on goal, and got a despairing hand on the ball as he fell over his own goal line. The Spurs players immediately claimed it had crossed the line, while Carroll insisted that he had clawed it to safety – referee Mark Clattenburg bafflingly refused to award the goal. Television replays showed it had gone at least two yards beyond the goal line and Jol's side had been robbed of the three points.

Jol and Spurs, however, had other things on their mind. Although he had signed a new, five-year contract twelve months earlier, Ledley and his advisers were now pushing for a much improved deal. His elevation to club captain demanded a renegotiation and his growing reputation as a fully-fledged international player had begun to attract interest from a host of leading English and European clubs, including Inter Milan in Italy and, if the rumour mill was to be believed, Arsenal.

'He loves Tottenham but, at the same time, Ledley needs to be playing for a club who match his ambitions,' his agent Jonathan Barnett told the *Daily Mail*. 'It's up to Tottenham, with their new manager, whether they can do that. They would have to break the bank to get him to sign another contract right now and that means the same kind of money being paid to other England defenders.

Spurs approached us with a tentative offer, but we're in no hurry.'

Ledley himself was eager to stress he was not holding the club to ransom. The skipper merely wanted a deal that reflected his new status and wanted reassurances that Spurs were continuing to plan for the future. 'The key to me staying at White Hart Lane is for the club to be challenging for trophies,' he admitted in the same *Daily Mail* article. 'We need to be moving in the right direction and, as long as we are doing that, there won't be a problem. The moment I feel that we are not is the time when I have to think about my future. It's flattering to be mentioned in the same breath as clubs like Arsenal and I can never say never but, at the same time, I don't want to think about leaving Spurs. As far as I'm concerned, I can achieve all my ambitions in the game at Tottenham.

'I have a young son to look after and I realise I have increased responsibilities on the pitch. Sometimes circumstances change and you look back and realise you have matured. There have been big changes in my life and, suddenly, I feel so much more responsible about everything and so much more grown-up.'

The contract negotiations would not be resolved until the following year but Ledley did not dwell on the off-field distraction as Spurs prepared for an FA Cup third-round clash with Brighton at White Hart Lane. Although climbing the Premiership table remained the priority, a good Cup run would be a morale-boosting exercise under the new managerial set-up and Jol's decision to field a full-strength line-up was clear evidence of the importance he attached to the competition.

It was not all plain sailing against the Championship side, however, and Spurs went in at half-time with a one-goal lead courtesy of Ledley's looping header from Reto Ziegler's cross. But his second goal of the season was not enough to subdue Brighton and they were on terms early in the second half when Richard Carpenter beat Paul Robinson with a curling 25-yard free-kick. Tottenham were frustrated until the 82nd minute but the wait for the winner proved worth it as Robbie Keane struck a spectacular volley into the top corner.

Defeats to Chelsea and Crystal Palace on the successive weekends in the league took some of the gloss of Jol's early successes, but the FA Cup continued to be a welcome distraction. West Brom were the fourth-round opponents at the Hawthorns and, although Tottenham were unable to despatch the Baggies on their patch, emerging with a 1–1 draw, they had no such problems in the replay a week later and booked their place in the next round with a 3–1 win.

The Premiership campaign continued with defeat at Bolton but, just as the word 'crisis' was beginning to rear its ugly head once again, the team produced a vintage performance against Portsmouth at the Lane in early February to dispel fears of a slump.

The hero on the day was Egyptian striker Mido, on an 18-month loan deal from Italian giants Roma, who marked his full début for the club with goals either side of half-time to help set up a much-needed 3–1 victory. Tottenham were back on track.

'We did need it, the last three games have been disappointing results for us, so we desperately wanted to win here,' the captain admitted after the game. 'We started the game really well and it was disappointing to concede from a set-piece – they weren't really in the game until they scored. After that, we had to dig a bit deeper, we played some good football and scored the equaliser. There was only going to be one team pushing on from there.

'Mido is a big, strong lad and he was lively. He wanted the ball, has good technical ability and can score goals – as he showed here. We are all happy for him and it is not bad scoring two goals in your first game.'

A day after the Pompey game, Sven-Göran Eriksson revealed his squad to face Holland in a friendly at Villa Park the following week. Rio Ferdinand and Sol Campbell were both ruled out with injury and Ledley looked certain to win his 11th cap until he, too, was forced to withdraw 24 hours later with a knee problem. It was not serious but the club were unwilling to risk their new skipper for a non-competitive fixture. Manchester United's Wes Brown was drafted in as cover and Ledley had no option but to put club before country.

The enforced rest again had the required recuperative effect and he was back in the side to play fallen giants Nottingham Forest in the fifth round of the Cup. The game was a replay of the iconic FA Cup Final of 1991 which Spurs won in extra-time thanks to a Des Walker own-goal, but 14 years later and with Forest languishing in the Championship, the smart money was on a Tottenham victory at the Lane.

By the end of the 90 minutes, however, it was Jol's men who could consider themselves fortunate still to be in the competition. Spurs huffed and puffed their way through the first half and were gifted a goal on the stroke of half-time when 19-year-old, on-loan goalkeeper Colin Doyle spilled Jermain Defoe's free-kick and had to watch helplessly as the ball trickled over the line. It was the softest of goals and one the home side barely deserved. Forest refused to feel sorry for themselves, though, and it was soon after the restart when Gareth Taylor tapped in from close range. Doyle redeemed himself for his first-half howler with a string of point-blank saves from Defoe and Mido and Spurs were heading for their second replay of the competition.

The good news was that the team were still in the hunt for silverware but the bad news was that Ledley was now struggling with a persistent groin problem. It wasn't, at this stage, serious enough to threaten his involvement for the rest of the season, but it was requiring constant treatment and the club were having to be increasingly mindful of his recovery after each match. 'I haven't been training so much with the groin problem,' he admitted. 'You can't think about that too much, though... Recently, I haven't been able to train early in the week after a game.'

As it transpired, the skipper was back for the 2–0 win over Fulham but missed the subsequent Cup replay against Forest. For once, though, the team did not miss his muscular presence and made a mockery of the stalemate in the first game with a 3–0 drubbing of the

Championship outfit. Spurs were safely through to the quarter-finals and expectations of a tenth appearance in the Final in the club's history were growing. Newcastle United at St James's Park stood in their way.

'It means a lot to me and it means a lot to the club,' Ledley told the Spurs website in the build-up to the big game. 'With the great history we have in the Cup, with the success, you get caught up in it as a young player here and it is something you want to be part of. Of course, with it being at St James' Park, there is going to be a lot of support for them. It will be hard, but we went there earlier in the season and got a good result. We can take that there with us.

'All the players and fans want to win it. You don't get too many opportunities and you can't take anything for granted, no matter what age you are. We have slowly progressed through and we're all feeling confident. We know Newcastle is going to be a tough game and a big game – we are really looking forward to it.

'Being captain and leading the team out gives you that extra little personal boost. I am really looking forward to it, everyone is. I can't wait for Sunday. We know it is a big game for us and, even though we have played it pretty low-key this week, all the players have got it in their thoughts.'

More than 50,000 fans roared the teams out on Tyneside and they had to wait a mere five minutes for the first goal of the game. Alan Shearer surged down the right and cut the ball back across the Spurs area where Dutch striker Patrick Kluivert was on hand to supply the finish. The majority of the crowd were in raptures and Jol's side already had a mountain to climb. Newcastle may have been the home side but spent the rest of the game on the back foot as Tottenham repeatedly knocked on the door but could find no way through. Freddie Kanouté, Simon Davies and Robbie Keane all went close, but the Magpies held firm and the semi-final place belonged to them.

'We bossed the game, really, and I think it was a game where if we had scored one, we would have gone on and won it,' the Spurs skipper said after the match. 'After playing so well, we are so disappointed to have got nothing from the game. It was a good performance by us, we had a lot of young players out there and Newcastle have got some experienced players. We dominated the game and that is not easy to do here – but they have won it.

'It's good to know we did everything we could, but we haven't won the game. That is the main thing – we want to be winners. We could take heart from the performance but it would have been nicer to have played badly and won.'

The league was now the club's sole focus and, with ten games to go before the end of the campaign, there was still the enticing prospect of UEFA Cup qualification and the lure of European football the following season.

Defeat to Charlton and victory over Manchester City kept the team in the hunt before the climax of the domestic season could unfold; there were also two more World Cup qualifiers for England to contend with at the end of March in the shape of Northern Ireland at Old Trafford and Azerbaijan at St James's Park. Sven-Göran Eriksson's side were on top of Group Six and six points from the two games would represent a huge step towards the World Cup finals in the summer of 2006.

When Eriksson announced the squad, there was no Sol Campbell, who was still sidelined by injury, and the battle for the centre-half places looked like a straight three-way fight between Ledley, John Terry and Rio Ferdinand. The latter two seemed to have the slight edge but the other two Spurs players in the England squad were quick to lend their support to their club captain. 'If you ask me who is the best defender in the world, then it's an interesting one, but I'm going to say an English defender, definitely,' Jermain Defoe told the FA website. 'I think Rio Ferdinand is up there but I always have to talk about Ledley King as well, because playing against him he is so consistent. I know playing against him in training is not the same as matches, but he plays the same every single game. He's strong, his awareness is fantastic and he reads the game so well.

'Against France in Euro 2004, he was brilliant against Thierry Henry... I think Henry didn't really have a chance. But there are so many good defenders in England because John Terry has been excellent as well. Those three English defenders are just unbelievable.'

Tottenham 'keeper Paul Robinson was equally loyal to his White Hart Lane team-mate. 'Ledley's done really well this season and has gone from strength to strength,' he said. 'He's a class act and has played well week in, week out. But we can all see the competition for centre-back places for England. Look at the squad and there are four top-class centre-halves in Ledley, Sol Campbell, Rio Ferdinand and John Terry. Picking two to play from that is almost unfair on the other two. It's a great position to be in for England, but I suppose it's unfortunate for Ledley, although I'm sure he'll win plenty of caps in his career.'

Unfortunately, Eriksson was not swayed and opted for Ferdinand and Terry. It was another disappointment for Ledley, but England's 4–0 victory over Northern Ireland in Manchester left little room for argument. The side selected by the coach had done the job and only injury to either of his central defenders would have persuaded him to change a winning line-up against Azerbaijan. Ledley duly took his place on the bench at St James's Park and England set out looking for their second victory in five days.

Azerbaijan proved surprisingly stubborn opponents in Newcastle. England laid siege to their goal in the opening 45 minutes but could find no way through. The anxiety levels only rose in the first five minutes of the second half as the sides remained deadlocked and there were audible sighs of relief around the ground when Steven Gerrard finally pierced the Azerbaijan defence on 51 minutes. David Beckham added the all-important second nine minutes later to seal the result and England were home and dry. Eriksson took advantage of the two-goal cushion to throw Ledley on for Ferdinand with little more than ten minutes left to win his 12th cap, but it was too little time for the Tottenham skipper to make any significant impact on proceedings.

The race for UEFA Cup qualification was at least a welcome distraction as he returned to White Hart Lane, and hopes of reaching Europe were boosted with a four-match unbeaten run that featured victory over Newcastle and draws with Birmingham, Liverpool and West Brom. It wasn't an irresistible sequence of results but it did keep Spurs firmly in the hunt.

A 1–0 defeat at Highbury in the north London derby was a significant setback but victory over Aston Villa in the next match would repair much of the damage. The Midlanders were also in contention for a UEFA Cup place and Ledley admitted as the game approached that the first taste of European football at White Hart Lane since 2000 was long overdue.

'When you're a teenager, maybe you don't realise how difficult it is to get into Europe and how limited the chances are,' Ledley said in an interview with the *Express*. 'You think maybe you'll win a cup here and there, or do it through your league position. But as time has gone on, I've realised Europe is something we've found difficult to get into and we're just striving to get back there this season.

'The new manager has come in and worked wonders, we've all gelled together, we're hungry and we would be really disappointed if we didn't make it this season. The chance is there for us now so we have to take it.

'We're a massive club and, with the players we've had over the years, you'd expect us to have challenged. But it's quite simple – we haven't done well enough. It's down to the players to do better. I remember being on the bench against Kaiserslautern [in the UEFA Cup in 2000] and, although it was quite intimidating for a young player, it was a great experience. But it wasn't enough and I'm desperate for some more.'

His desperation was there for all to see against Villa as Spurs ran riot. Ledley forced goalkeeper Stefan Postma into a fine save after just two minutes, but the visitors drew some breathing space for only another four minutes before Freddie Kanouté crashed home the opener. Ledley got his goal on 19 minutes when he capitalised on indecision in the Villa defence and poked home from close range. Spurs were flying and a second goal from Kanouté, plus strikes from Andy Reid and Stephen Kelly, sealed a handsome 5–1 victory. There were two games remaining and all to play for.

The penultimate game of the season was at the Riverside against Middlesbrough, who sat above Spurs in the table, but the elation that followed the demolition of Villa quickly turned to despair as 'Boro grabbed an early lead through George Boateng and then kept Tottenham at bay at the other end.

Victory for Middlesbrough meant they needed only a single point from their last game of the season at Manchester City to wrap up seventh place and claim the final UEFA Cup place. Spurs, in contrast, had to beat Blackburn Rovers at White Hart Lane and hope and pray that City did them a favour.

It would have been a fairytale ending but ultimately it

failed to materialise. Middlesbrough come away from Eastlands with their all-important point following a 1–1 draw, while Tottenham were unable to find a way past Blackburn and, despite the vociferous support of the Lane faithful, the game finished as a goalless draw. The European dream was over and Spurs would have yet another summer break to reflect on what might have been.

'It was frustrating... they got bodies behind the ball and it was difficult for us to break them down,' Ledley admitted as the season finally drew to an anti-climactic close. 'We knew it would be like that and we struggled with it.

'It was a difficult situation to go into and we were concentrating on trying to get the win. If you score one in good time, you can push on, but we didn't want to go gung-ho and had to be disciplined in our performance. Blackburn played well, there was no pressure on them and they have improved a lot since Mark Hughes took over. They are a hard team to break down.'

Spurs finished ninth, which was an improvement on the previous season, but there was no great celebratory mood within the club. European football had eluded them once again and, whatever the strides the side had made under Jol, they had not achieved a top-six finish.

On a personal level, however, the season had been Ledley's best at the club. Despite nursing his ongoing groin problems, he had featured in all 38 of the team's Premiership games. In fact, he missed just one of the side's total of 48 league and Cup outings – he was rested for the FA Cup replay with Forest – and his consistent quality saw him rewarded with the club captaincy and a new contract. He was now Tottenham's longest-serving player and the figurehead of the team out on the pitch and the club as a whole. He had already come a long way since his nerve-wracked début as an 18-year-old against Liverpool seven years ago.

The push for European qualification would resume next season. For now, Ledley was heading for a well-earned holiday. The England squad was flying to the United States for friendlies against America and Colombia but the Spurs skipper widely decided discretion was the better part of valour and opted to rest his weary body.

'It would have been a nice trip but, with the groin problems I've had this season that are still playing up, I think it is probably the best thing to miss out,' he said. 'It is disappointing but I have to do the right thing for my body and we decided the best thing was to stay behind. A break will be nice as it is the first time I have managed to go through a season without missing any games. I am feeling the strain of that a little bit now and the rest will be good. Touch wood, I'll come back, and have a good season.'

7

A NEW HOPE

Spurs supporters had good reason to believe that the 2005/06 season would finally be the year their team made the breakthrough to the upper echelons of the Premiership. A decade of underachievement and disappointment had not unduly dulled the level of expectation in N17 and, although the fans had experienced more than their fair share of false dawns, there now seemed to be genuine grounds for optimism.

Martin Jol had inherited the manager's job from Jacques Santini unexpectedly the previous season and, once the affable Dutchman had come to terms with his sudden promotion, there were signs he was taking the team in the right direction. The new season would be his first full campaign and he had now had time to stamp his mark on the side, the coaching set-up and the players themselves.

And then there was Ledley. Like Jol, he had been 'promoted' mid-season, taking the captaincy in the wake of Jamie Redknapp's New Year move to Southampton, and he'd had precious little time to adapt to his new role as the unforgiving football calendar ensured the fixtures came thick and fast. The new season would see the 24-year-old in situ from the start and that, too, boded well for Tottenham's fortunes.

On the transfer front, the club persisted with its policy of trying to sign young British talent and, over the summer, the squad was bolstered by the arrival of Jermaine Jenas from Newcastle, highly-rated Leeds winger Aaron Lennon, talented Derby midfielder Tom Huddlestone and Crystal Palace wide-man Wayne Routledge. All were players with a bright future ahead of them and the Tottenham squad was looking increasingly vibrant and youthful.

There was, however, still room for a few old heads to help guide the teenagers and 20-somethings through the rigours of the upcoming season. Wily old Finnish campaigner Teemu Tainio was signed from Auxerre on a free and the club pulled off a major coup when veteran Dutch midfielder Edgar Davids agreed to join after leaving Inter Milan. The squad was now in place for the assault on the top six.

The only cloud on the horizon was Ledley's groin problem. Although he was fit enough to fly out with the team for the Peace Cup in South Korea in July and played in the 3–1 victory over Lyon in the Final in Seoul, the injury was continuing to bother him and, when Spurs returned to London to complete their pre-season preparations, he was still in some discomfort. He played in the friendly against Reading at the Madejski Stadium but missed Tottenham's final pre-season match against Porto at White Hart Lane. The clash with the Portuguese was just a week before the season opener against Portsmouth at Fratton Park and there were now real concerns that he wouldn't be ready for the Pompey game. Both the player and his manager were determined to remain positive about the injury but the suspicion was that Ledley would miss the start of the season.

'It's fine,' Ledley told the club website. 'I've got to work on it and strengthen it all the time. I managed to play through last season but did have a few problems and I don't want the same this season – I want it to be right. I might have to miss the odd session in training to make sure it is all OK for the new season. Last season was the first time I have played all the games and I want to do it again. I must make sure everything is right now to give me the best chance of doing that.'

Jol was equally insistent his captain would be ready to play on the south coast. 'It's not serious,' the Dutchman said. 'You always have to wait and see how we cope when he's not playing because I think he's our most important player. He will play against Portsmouth.'

Unfortunately, the pair's confidence was to prove misplaced and Ledley was forced to sit out the team's first four league games. In his absence, Spurs beat Portsmouth and Middlesbrough and drew with Blackburn before their Chelsea jinx struck yet again and they were beaten 2–0 by the Blues at White Hart Lane. His enforced lay-off also meant missing England's friendly with Denmark in Copenhagen and their two World Cup qualifiers with Northern Ireland and Wales but, by early September, he was poised for a return to the trenches. The international break had given him an extra week to recover and, as Tottenham's clash with Liverpool at the Lane loomed, he was almost ready.

'In the last couple of days, I have got back into training and done about 45 minutes each day,' he said in the week before the match. 'It has gone well... I expected to feel some reaction but there is nothing I can't manage at the moment. The break buys me a bit of time and, hopefully, it will mean I don't miss another game. Now is the time to get it right and make sure I come back strong – that is what I am going to do.'

With his groin on the mend, Jol had no hesitation restoring his captain to the starting line-up and it looked as if he had never been away as he and Anthony Gardener shackled Reds strikers Peter Crouch and Djibril Cissé with ease. At the other end, both Jermain Defoe and new signing Grzegorz Rasiak had 'goals' ruled out for Spurs and the game finished goalless. It may not have been the three points Jol wanted, but Ledley came through unscathed, which in itself was a huge bonus.

A shock League Cup loss to Grimsby was the lowlight of September but few fans were grumbling as the team's league form continued to impress. Spurs were held at Aston Villa, but victories over London rivals Fulham and Charlton – in which Ledley scored his ninth goal for the club – were evidence of a growing confidence and ability to win crucial games. October had only just begun but Tottenham already looked like a more resilient yet still dangerous outfit.

Ledley's return to first-team action was just in time to catch Sven-Göran Eriksson's eye. England's qualifying campaign had stuttered with a shock 1–0 defeat to Northern Ireland in Belfast in September and the upcoming games against Austria and Poland had now taken on a far greater importance. Ledley had club five games under his belt following his groin problems and, with the Swede needing to select his strongest squad possible, he was quick to recall the Spurs skipper into the international fold.

The Austria clash was the first of an Old Trafford double-header and Eriksson opted to pair Sol Campbell with John Terry in the centre of the defence, while Ledley and Rio Ferdinand had to content themselves with a place among the substitutes.

The Austrians had held England just over a year ago in Vienna and the game in Manchester was equally frustrating for Eriksson's side as the visitors once again acquitted themselves well against their more celebrated opponents. England probed and prodded but got little joy from the Austrian defence and their breakthrough on 25 minutes came courtesy of a penalty. Michael Owen surged into the area and was hacked down by Paul Scharner and the Spanish referee pointed to the spot. Frank Lampard took responsibility and put England ahead with a well-struck penalty.

The goal failed to imbue England with either the confidence or ambition to go for the Austrian jugular and it was still 1–0 on the hour when disaster struck. David Beckham had been booked just two minutes earlier for a foul on full-back Andreas Ibertsberger and then senselessly dived in on the same player to earn himself a second yellow card and an early bath. In the process, he became the first player to be sent off twice in an England career and, with Austria far from dead and buried, and Eriksson's team down to ten men, nerves were beginning to fray.

After the débâcle in Belfast, Eriksson could ill afford to lose the game. His first instinct was to look to his bench and he decided to take off Joe Cole and introduce Ledley. The Swede was prepared to sacrifice Cole's creativity and sent Ledley out with strict instructions to sit in front of the back four and stifle the Austrian attacks at their source. Ledley's versatility was, this time, a virtue and he followed his orders to the letter as England's ten men held firm and held on for a patchy 1–0 win that booked their place at the World Cup.

'It was nervy, but it was always going to be when you play with 10 men for around 35 minutes,' a relieved Eriksson said at full-time. 'We suffered but we did it together. Austria were physically a very strong team and put in a lot of long, high balls, but we defended brilliantly and fought all together as a team.'

With Beckham suspended for the Poland game four days later and Steven Gerrard and Sol Campbell ruled out through injury, the coach had some testing selection issues to resolve. Terry needed a new partner in the heart of the defence and two of the midfield quartet who had started against Austria were unavailable. Victory over Poland would guarantee England top spot in their qualifying group and Eriksson knew he had to get it right, especially as the Poles were likely to show more adventure than Austria going forward.

'I know it is different and it will be a more open game for sure because Poland will not defend like Austria,' Eriksson admitted before the game. 'They will not defend with nine men behind the ball every time they lose possession.'

When the time came to make his decision, the Swede decided to recall Ferdinand in the middle of the back four and, once again, asked Ledley to play the holding midfield role. Chelsea's Shaun Wright-Phillips took the second vacant midfield spot and a new-look England were ready.

Perhaps it was the knowledge that their place at the World Cup the following summer was already assured or perhaps it was the enforced change in personnel, but England looked a different side from the one that had laboured against Austria and, from the start, they looked fluid, confident and dangerous. With Ledley, who was celebrating his 25th birthday, giving the rest of the midfield the licence to attack further upfield, England enjoyed the bulk of possession and created the lion's share of the chances. The inevitable first breakthrough was only a matter of time and, although England had to wait until a minute before the break to get it, Michael Owen's 33rd goal for England was no more than their performance deserved.

Poland did stun the home crowd just seconds later with an equaliser courtesy of a fierce volley from Tomasz Frankowski – the last kick of the half – but England were not to be denied and came out for the second period in determined mood. They dominated the subsequent 45 minutes and victory was duly sealed 10 minutes from the final whistle when Lampard applied the finish to an incisive counter-attack. The result saw England emphatically leapfrog the Poles into top spot in the group and Eriksson and his side were able to reflect on a job well done.

For Ledley, the match had been a triumph. Poland scored with their one and only meaningful attack but, that aside, the Spurs captain had been utterly dominant in the holding role as his natural, languid athleticism and cultured distribution shone through. The team were heading to the World Cup finals, but much of the post-match discussion still centred on the Tottenham star and a performance, albeit in a different position, to rival his Euro 2004 display against France.

'Ledley King came on and did very well against Austria on Saturday and played excellently again today,' Eriksson enthused. 'You can see he is very useful in that role, he's strong and very good on the ball. He's another option and it's very good to have many options when you know that next summer you will play a lot of games in a short space of time.'

The BBC's Alan Hansen agreed. 'King was fantastic in the holding midfield role – better than I thought he could possibly play,' he wrote on the BBC website. 'He showed excellent positional sense and he was disciplined and he wasn't bad on the ball either. Looking at his performance tonight, he has a decent chance of making the position his own.'

Of course, Ledley himself was the epitome of modesty after the game when the plaudits started flying his way. 'I spoke to the manager before the game about my role, so I knew beforehand. It's something I had done for a little while, so I was quite comfortable with it,' he told the FA website. 'The holding role is quite a bit different. Playing at the back, you see everything in front of you... playing in midfield, you receive the ball from the back. You have your back to the play which never really happens as a defender, but it's something I have done a few times in my career so far and I've quite enjoyed it, so I haven't got a problem.

'I'll leave it to other people to judge if I keep playing well for my club and if I get the chance with my country to play at the back. It's just great to be in the squad. I've missed the last few so it's great to be back in. To get on the pitch is great for me also. If I can do that by playing different positions, I'm happy to do that.

'I was trying to just sit in there and break things up as much as possible and give it to the players who can play. I try to sit in there as much as possible and give Frank [Lampard] the freedom to go on and do what he's great at. You've seen that with the way he's taken the goal. With me there, hopefully, he felt he could push on and just leave me to pick up the pieces.

'Overall, I felt I did well, but I've always said I've never given up on centre-back. I still feel that I could do a job there. The next few months will be interesting and we will see what happens. We'll see what the manager wants from me and go from there.'

Ledley returned to White Hart Lane with the widespread plaudits ringing in his ears and, with their captain on the top of his game, the club's new signings continuing to impress and Martin Jol clearly enjoying the manager's job, Spurs were on a roll. Between the Everton game in mid-October and the clash with Birmingham on Boxing Day, they went ten league games with just one defeat.

That loss came at the Reebok against Bolton but the run also included a battling 1–1 draw at Old Trafford against Manchester United, and the same result against Arsenal at the Lane, when Ledley seemed to have won the match with his second goal of the season, only for Robert Pires to snatch a point for the Gunners with a late equaliser. There was also his 15th cap for his country in mid-November when he again took the holding midfield role in a 3–2 win over Argentina in Geneva and his third goal of the season in the 3–1 win over Portsmouth in December – his 190th senior game for the club. In short, life for Ledley and Spurs was extremely good. The run took the side into the top four – above arch-rivals Arsenal – and suddenly the club were now thinking about Champions League rather than UEFA Cup qualification.

It was a spectacular turnaround in fortunes after so many travails over the previous seasons but, perhaps, it was just a little too good to be true and, while the 2–0 victory over Birmingham at White Hart Lane cemented the side's place in the rarefied atmosphere of the top four, the win came with a price. Spurs were one up and coasting in the second half when Ledley went down clutching his groin and, as he hobbled off the pitch to be replaced by Noé Pamarot, everyone at the Lane feared the worst.

The injury was to cost him three weeks of the season but, by mid-January, he had recovered sufficiently to be hopeful of playing against Liverpool at Anfield. 'I have only just started to run in the last two days, but my injury feels OK and I don't think my fitness has suffered too much,' he told the club website in the days leading up to the clash on Merseyside. 'If I can build it up more throughout the week then, hopefully, I can be involved. The signs are good at the moment. I missed the first four games of the season and came back against Liverpool – and it looks like it could be the same again after missing another four. It is quite strange.'

Spurs had held the Reds in north London earlier in the season but they could not repeat the trick at Anfield, despite another assured performance. Harry Kewell grabbed the only goal of the match in the second half and Paul Stalteri was sent off late on, but Ledley came through the 90 minutes without aggravating the injury and Tottenham steeled themselves for the all-important run-in and their bid to qualify for Europe.

The next five games were to prove inconclusive. Although they lost only once – a heartbreaking 1–0 defeat at Fulham thanks to an injury-time winner for the Cottagers – they also only won once, beating

Charlton 3–1 at the Lane. The team were still in the top four but the chasing pack, headed by Arsenal, were closing in ominously.

The Premiership, however, was briefly put on hold for the England friendly against Uruguay at Anfield at the start of March. It was to be a temporary respite from the intense pressure of the race for Europe and, although he was on the bench for the first half against the South Americans, Sven-Göran Eriksson gave him the whole of the second period in the heart of the defence alongside Rio Ferdinand.

Uruguay had taken the lead in the 26th minute through midfielder Omar Pouso but with Ledley at the back, England did not concede again and snatched victory with goals from Peter Crouch on 75 minutes and a last-gasp winner from Joe Cole.

Ledley had again looked very much at home on the international stage and there was a growing consensus that the Spurs skipper had done enough to force his way into Eriksson's starting line-up. 'A solid no-thrills display,' was the verdict of the BBC website. 'Looks comfortable in an England shirt and, given Sol Campbell's problems and Rio Ferdinand's indifferent form, he could yet force his way into the reckoning.'

England's next fixture was not until the end of May against Hungary, leaving Ledley and his international team-mates free to return to their clubs and concentrate on the final eleven league games of the campaign. First up for Spurs were Blackburn at White Hart Lane and, after the side's recent stutters, their 3–2 victory in a five-goal thriller was greeted with relief by Martin Jol and his players.

Six days later, the team travelled to west London to face Chelsea looking for their first league win over the Blues for 16 years. It was to be another major landmark in Ledley's career with the captain making his 200th senior appearance for the club and he hoped to celebrate it with a rare victory and, more importantly in the context of Tottenham's season, three priceless points.

It was Chelsea, however, who made the first breakthrough after fourteen minutes when Ghanaian midfielder Michael Essien scored from close range, but the new-look Spurs were not prepared to lie down and were back on terms on the stroke of half-time when Jermaine Jenas latched on to Michael Dawson's header and beat Petr Cech.

The second half was tight and both sides had their chances. Tottenham's best fell to Jenas, who broke clear after Ledley's slide-rule pass but he was unable to beat Cech for a second time. The match seemed destined for an honourable draw until French defender William Gallas collected the ball on the edge of the Spurs area in injury time and unleashed an unstoppable drive that gave Paul Robinson no chance. Tottenham had been robbed of the point their performance deserved and Ledley's 200th game ended in bitter disappointment.

'We came up against the best team in the country and most people would say we deserved something from the game,' Spurs coach Chris Hughton said. 'We started very bright, did well on the counter-attack and, in the second half, we looked solid and coped fairly well. It was heartbreaking but we're still upbeat about finishing in fourth place.'

The team bounced back from their Stamford Bridge blow with back-to-back wins over Birmingham and West Brom to stay in fourth place and, although they lost 3–1 at Newcastle – a game which Ledley was forced to sit out with an ankle knock – they remained in charge of their own destiny. Victories over Manchester City and Everton strengthened their position but disaster struck in the match at Goodison Park, leaving the club and their inspirational captain in a state of shock.

Tottenham took the lead at Everton on the half-hour courtesy of a Robbie Keane penalty and, as the clock ticked down in the second half, Spurs were heading for a crucial win. But before the final whistle, Ledley was forced to hobble off the pitch wincing in pain after a clash with striker Duncan Ferguson and, by the pained look on his face, it was obvious it was a serious injury.

The next day, the club confirmed what everyone feared – Ledley had suffered a stress fracture to the fourth metatarsal of his left foot. His season was over. The news was a devastating blow for the player, his club and his country. Spurs had four games left in which to secure fourth place and the lucrative prize of Champions League football the following season, and they would have to do it without their talismanic captain. For England, the injury was equally disastrous. The World Cup in Germany was looming large and it was now touch and go whether the bone would heal in time for him to make the squad.

'He won't play for the next three weeks,' Jol said after the match. 'Hopefully, he can be fit between now and the first week in May. You have to assess it every week but I think he has a good chance [of being fit for the World Cup].'

Typically, Ledley took the news philosophically and his thoughts were firmly fixed on Tottenham's plight rather than his own personal agenda. 'It is an exciting time for the club and one that I was looking forward to,' said the central defender. 'It is what you want to be involved in coming up to the end of the season, big games against Manchester United, Arsenal, Bolton and West Ham – games that we need points from.'

The game at Old Trafford proved how far Spurs had progressed. Even without their skipper, Jol's side were dominant for long periods in Manchester and, ultimately, the difference between the two teams was Wayne Rooney who scored twice in the first half. Jermaine Jenas pulled one back for Tottenham but it was not enough and they headed back empty-handed to north London in preparation for the derby with Arsenal.

The stakes could not have been higher at Highbury. There were, of course, the usual old scores to settle but there was also the race for fourth place and it was the final game at the old stadium before the Gunners relocated to the Emirates. Rarely had a derby had so much riding on it.

Again, Spurs showed why they had been in fourth place in the table since the New Year with a confident and resilient display and they took the lead after 66 minutes when Robbie Keane netted from close range. Arsenal predictably came storming back and they finally found the equaliser from Thierry Henry six minutes from the end. There was still time for Edgar Davids to get sent off which set up a dramatic five final minutes, but Jol's team held their ground and a point apiece was infinitely more welcome news to Spurs than it was to their old rivals.

A 1–0 victory over Bolton at the Lane thanks to Aaron Lennon's 60th-minute strike in the penultimate game of the season meant that if the team beat West Ham at Upton Park a week later, they were guaranteed fourth place and Champions League football. If Arsenal lost to Wigan on the same day, the result at West Ham was irrelevant.

It was agonising for Ledley to watch events unfold in front of him and have no involvement in proceedings but, as the Hammers clash approached, the team were in confident mood. On the eve of the game, however, the squad were staying at an east London hotel close to Upton Park and, after eating their evening meal together, ten of the players fell sick. Later tests were to show they had not fallen victim to food poisoning, as had been initially suspected, but that was little consolation to Jol and his coaching staff as they contemplated fielding a side that wasn't physically up to the job.

In desperation, Spurs asked the Premiership for a 24-hour postponement to the fixture to allow the players – including Robbie Keane, Michael Dawson, Aaron Lennon and Michael Carrick – to recover, but their request was turned down. They would have to play the game or risk a punitive and potentially disastrous points deduction.

Six of the players who took to the field at Upton Park had been laid low the night before and some were vomiting in the dressing room before kick-off. It was the biggest game in the club's recent history and half the team should have been in their sick beds.

West Ham started brightly and took the lead on ten minutes through Welsh international Carl Fletcher, but Spurs dug deep into their reserves and were back on level terms 35 minutes later when Jermain Defoe showed his class with a superb finish after he was put through by Michael Carrick. It was all square at half-time but Arsenal were being held 2–2 by Wigan at Highbury and, if the two games stayed that way, Tottenham were still heading for the Champions League.

The second 45 minutes at Upton Park began to take their toll on the visitors and the Hammers were by far the more energetic side. Spurs clung on but were visibly on the ropes and ten minutes from time Yossi Benayoun found space after a corner and fired home the winner. Jol and his players could only hope Wigan pulled off a shock at Highbury, but it was not to be and it was Arsenal and not Tottenham who finished fourth and booked their place in the Champions League.

'We asked to postpone the game for 24 hours but we didn't want to risk sanctions,' Jol said. 'We took a gamble but I think you saw we weren't strong enough. I can appreciate the reasons we could not postpone it. West Ham didn't want to play on Monday because they have the FA Cup Final on Saturday. It's always a thought that maybe we could have done better with a fit squad, but I have to say to myself that it's all in the game. We're in Europe and that's the main target but to be fourth for most of the season and to lose it on the last day is a big disappointment.'

It was a heartbreaking end to the campaign but there was also much to celebrate. Spurs had qualified for the UEFA Cup, their first taste of European football since 1999, and their fifth place was the club's highest placed top-flight finish for 16 years. The unexpected possibility of a place in the Champions League only for to the team to be denied on the final day of the season briefly cast a shadow over the other achievements but, on balance, it had been a high-achieving nine months for the club.

The day after the West Ham heartbreak, Sven-Göran Eriksson named his World Cup squad. Tottenham proudly provided four of the 23 lucky players but while Aaron Lennon, Paul Robinson, Jermaine Jenas and Michael Carrick could now look forward to playing a part in the biggest football tournament on the planet, Ledley had to come to terms with the bleak reality that his broken metatarsal had cost him his place. He had not played since the Everton game in mid-April and Eriksson, understandably, could not take the risk on him. There was just no way to accelerate the healing process and Ledley had to accept that his World Cup dream was over.

There was, however, one ray of light in the gloom. Ledley's contract negotiations had been going on for over a year but just days before Eriksson confirmed he wasn't taking Ledley to Germany, Spurs were finally able to announce that their captain had signed a four-year contract extension. 'The new deal has taken a while to sort out, but there was never any question about me staying,' Ledley said after putting pen to paper. 'I want to continue captaining this club in what is hopefully going to be a very successful period.'

It was the news all Tottenham fans had been desperately waiting to hear and Ledley and the club could now plan for the future and build on what had been their best season for more than a decade.

The summer of 2006 was no holiday for Ledley. While Spurs' international contingent were plying their trade for their respective countries at the World Cup and the rest of the squad were on the beach, the club captain was back on the training ground tentatively testing out his broken foot.

By the time his team-mates reported back for pre-season training in July, he was ready to fly to France for the club's training camp and, although he wasn't risked in the friendly against Bordeaux, Martin Jol decided to start him in the next game against Nice and his skipper enjoyed an untroubled 70 minutes of action. The left foot came through unscathed and he could now look forward to a full pre-season and the new Premiership campaign.

'It was nice to be back out there, to get some minutes under my belt and, most importantly, to get through the game with no problems,' he told the club website after his successful comeback. 'It's been a long time, especially over the summer, watching all the games in the World

Cup. It was great to be back and playing with the lads again. It was a disappointing end to the season both for me personally in terms of the injury and the team just missing out on fourth place. I then had the disappointment with England as well. All these things make you stronger and, next season, I'm determined to bounce back and enjoy another good season at Spurs.'

Further friendlies against Celta Vigo, Birmingham and the club's traditional warm-up game with Stevenage all followed with Ledley in the starting line-up and looking fitter and stronger by the match but, at the end of July, his injury jinx struck once again. The defender damaged his knee in training and scans quickly revealed he had a cartilage injury that would keep him out for up to eight weeks. The knee required minor surgery and, for the second successive season, he was destined to miss the start of the campaign.

The club, meanwhile, were busy adding more players to the squad in anticipation of a two-pronged assault on domestic honours and Europe. Ivory Coast midfielder Didier Zokora, who had impressed in the summer at the World Cup, was signed from St Etienne for £8.2 million; Mido's loan deal from Roma was made permanent; and French full-back Pascal Chimbonda was lured away from Wigan in a £4.5 million deal. But the highest profile transfer was that of Bulgarian striker Dimitar Berbatov for £10.9 million from Bundesliga side Bayer Leverkusen. Michael Carrick joined Manchester United for £18.6 million but, on the balance of the summer's ins and outs, Tottenham looked to have significantly strengthened their resources.

Without the services of Ledley, Spurs made a faltering start to the new season. An opening day defeat to Bolton at the Reebok was followed by a 2–0 win over newly-promoted Sheffield United at the Lane but, no sooner had the side bagged their first three points of the campaign, they lost at home to Everton and, with Manchester United next up at Old Trafford, they were desperate for Ledley's leadership on the pitch.

The knee surgery in August had been a complete success and, although he had yet to play for the reserves, Jol decided the time was right for the team's talisman to return against United. Tottenham looked like a team reborn with the skipper marshalling the back four and the visitors were decidedly unlucky not to come away from Old Trafford with a share of the points. The only goal of the game came after just nine minutes when Paul Robinson was unable to hold a vicious Cristiano Ronaldo free-kick and the evergreen Ryan Giggs headed home. United made the most of their slice of luck but, that aside, they could find no way past Ledley and the rest of the Spurs defence and the captain was only denied an equaliser in the second-half by Edwin van der Sar's athleticism in goal. Jol decided to substitute Ledley with nine minutes left as Tottenham pushed for the equaliser, but his comeback had gone better than perhaps even he had dared hope.

'We haven't started the season well but, as soon as we have a settled team, we will get better and better, I'm sure of that,' Jol said after the game in reference to Ledley's impressive return. 'I felt we could have had a result. In the last two seasons, we've done well at Old Trafford and managed two good results – two draws – and we never gave a lot of chances away. This time we maybe gave away three or four but, on the other hand, I can recall five or six possibilities for us and that's the only disappointment. If you create five or six chances you should score, but we didn't, so that's the frustrating thing.'

There was little time to dwell on the disappointment. Five days later, Spurs were in action in the first round of the UEFA Cup away to dangerous Czech Republic side Slavia Prague and, after the club's seven-year absence from European competition, there was a real sense of anticipation. Tottenham's most recent taste of European football had been a bitter-sweet one after going out to German side Kaiserslautern in 1999 when they conceded twice in injury time with a place in the third round of the UEFA Cup beckoning. A 19-year-old Ledley had sat on the Spurs bench for the first leg against the Germans that year and, as he prepared this time for a long overdue chance finally to play in the competition, he reflected on Spurs' European aspirations for the season and his seemingly relentless injury woes. 'It's not been the start we thought of but, on a personal note, I'm just glad to be back out there playing,' he said before the game. 'It's been a long time. The European tie might be a nice way to take our minds off the league but I can tell you all the lads are hungry for European success. We've looked at what Middlesbrough achieved last season in reaching the Final and are thinking, "Why not?" It's been a long, hard road to get back into Europe and I must admit when I sat on the bench against Kaiserslautern six years ago, I was thinking we'd play in Europe every week.'

Ledley added that he'd managed to stay positive throughout his battle with injuries, and felt that his luck simply had to change. The hardest part of it all had been missing out on the World Cup, but he now had the opportunity to play in one of the most prestigious tournaments in European football, and he was relishing the prospect.

A modest crowd of 15,000 filled the Stadion Evzena Rosickeho in Prague for the first leg and Spurs betrayed their European inexperience with an uncharacteristically anxious performance and were indebted to Jermaine Jenas' well-taken goal after 37 minutes to steady the nerves. It was the only goal of the game and while the side's first foray on the Continent had hardly revived memories of the club's glorious European nights of years gone by, they came home with a first-leg advantage and the UEFA Cup campaign was finally up and running.

Back on the domestic front, the team continued to stutter and a goalless draw with Fulham at the Lane and a heavy 3–0 defeat against Liverpool at Anfield thrust Jol and the team into an unwanted media spotlight as critics began to question whether last season's impressive performances had merely been a flash in the pan. The team badly needed a morale-boosting victory.

The opportunity arose with the visit of Slavia Prague to the Lane for the second leg of their UEFA Cup tie. An aggregate victory over the Czechs would send Spurs through to the group stages of the competition and a guarantee of four more European games over the season and, although it was still only mid-September, it had become a must-win match. Sadly, Ledley's knee had become slightly swollen and he was rested, leaving Spurs to produce the result they badly needed without their skipper.

It was, in truth, another far-from-convincing European performance but Robbie Keane struck ten minutes from time to give Tottenham a 1–0 win on the night and a 2–0 aggregate victory. It was mission accomplished.

The first-leg victory over Slavia had failed to give the team a domestic boost but, this time, their European triumph did appear to infuse the side with much-needed confidence and, with Ledley back in the ranks for the visit of Portsmouth, they were finally back to winning ways in the league with a 2–1 triumph that steadied the ship.

'It's a game we knew we had to win,' the captain admitted after the game. 'I spoke to JJ [Jermaine Jenas] before the game and we agreed that we wanted to start quickly and how it would be great to go 1–0 up because we hadn't scored for a few league games. We knew if we scored that first goal it would put us in a strong position. We came out of the blocks quickly and scored early, exactly what we talked about beforehand. We felt we needed to start well, put pressure on them and we did that. It was a great start. We were a little edgy at times, we had to dig deep at times and didn't always play the most attractive football, but we got the three points.'

Spurs, however, would have to wait to see if they could continue the revival. Under new head coach Steve

McClaren, England faced back-to-back European Championship qualifiers against Macedonia and Croatia in October and the Premiership shut down as international football took centre-stage. Ledley had last pulled on an England shirt in March of that year in the friendly against Uruguay and, although his display against the South Americans had earned him a raft of plaudits, his inclusion in the squad was far from certain. Former England boss Sven-Göran Eriksson had been a self-declared admirer of Ledley's talent and versatility but the Spurs captain could not be sure McClaren shared the same view.

He need not have worried. The recently installed England coach had no hesitation in recalling him to the squad to join Tottenham team-mates Paul Robinson, Jermaine Jenas and Jermain Defoe but, having missed so much football over the past twelve months, he was unable to persuade McClaren to break up his first-choice pairing of John Terry and Rio Ferdinand in the heart of the defence and, once again, it seemed he would watch an England game from the bench. But then fate intervened and Ledley found himself pressed into action at the eleventh hour.

On the Saturday morning of the match at Old Trafford, Ferdinand reported a problem with his back to the England medical staff and McClaren decided not to risk the Manchester United centre-half. He immediately turned to Ledley and the Spurs skipper stepped out for the national anthems to win his 17th cap. His late inclusion was to prove England's salvation.

England were expected to roll over the Macedonians without much ado but the visitors proved stubborn opposition who were also more than capable of threatening attacking play, and the home side laboured throughout. Gary Neville and Steven Gerrard both hit the woodwork but England lacked conviction in the final third and Macedonia had their fair share of chances at the other end. Had it not been for a virtuoso performance from Ledley at the back, they could well have snatched a shock victory.

The post-match verdict was unanimous – Ledley was the only choice as Man of the Match. His seven-month absence from the international stage had done nothing to dim his effectiveness and, even with Ferdinand looking likely to be fit to face Croatia the following Wednesday, the consensus was that the Spurs man had to start in Zagreb.

'On a frustrating night for the Three Lions the biggest consolation for head coach Steve McClaren was another clean sheet and a strong performance from last-minute call-up Ledley King,' was the verdict of the FA website. 'King answered McClaren's late call when Rio Ferdinand woke up this morning with a back problem and the Tottenham man performed stoically for his country.'

BBC pundit Alan Hansen was equally impressed. 'Macedonia played well and had the better chances and, with a little more composure, they could have scored and you have to give them credit,' he conceded. 'England, in contrast, played poorly and never controlled the game. They looked devoid of structure and shape and it tells you something when your best player is Ledley King. His positional play was outstanding and he showed again that he is a magnificent centre-back.'

The *Sun*'s Mark Irwin simply wrote, 'King was drafted in as a last-minute replacement for the injured Rio Ferdinand against Macedonia and saved McClaren's bacon with a series of crucial covering tackles.'

Once again, Ledley had proven himself entirely at home in an England shirt. He had overcome the disappointment of not initially making the starting line-up and shown, even with such little time to prepare, that he was worthy of a place in the side on merit. 'I had to get my focus very quickly and prepare myself to play in a game in which I hadn't been expecting to start,' he admitted. 'I was aware that Rio was having a bit of a problem on Friday night and realised there was a chance that I might play instead. But I was only told for certain on the Saturday morning and I'm glad that we've come through with another clean sheet, even if the result wasn't what we hoped for.' He added that many would have thought that Macedonia would be a push-over, but he and the England team had known that they would probably play with a great deal of resilience and skill. However 'inferior' the team appeared on paper in the group stages of the European Championships, such games would always be hard-fought affairs, and shocks were always a possibility. The three games coming up would be similarly testing – Croatia, Israel and Andorra – and Ledley felt that it would be quite an achievement qualifying from the group. And in order to do that, England needed to raise their game. They had not played well against Macedonia and, if they were going to get anything from the away leg in Croatia, then the team would have to perform.

The England coach now faced a major dilemma. Ferdinand was declared fit for the Croatia game but there would have been uproar if he dared to drop Ledley. In the end, however, the decision was taken out of his hands. Ledley's knee flared up again two days after the Macedonia stalemate and, although it was not considered unduly serious, McClaren and Spurs decided to be cautious and he returned to White Hart Lane for treatment while the rest of the squad flew out to Zagreb. The injury had robbed him of what had appeared to be a prolonged run in the England side.

It was bitter pill to swallow for the self-effacing player. He was forced to watch the Croatia game at home on the television and he celebrated his 26th birthday two days later in the knowledge that he would not be fit for resumption of the league campaign at Aston Villa at the weekend. It was a bleak time but the club captain refused to feel sorry for himself and he battled his way to fitness. His comeback would be in the UEFA Cup against Turkish side Besiktas and his return to the team would be the catalyst for a remarkable upturn in fortunes.

Tottenham had drawn with Villa to make it three games unbeaten and, with Ledley back in the ranks, the team went from strength to strength. Besiktas were beaten 2–0 in Istanbul thanks to goals either side of half-time from Egyptian midfielder Hossam Ghaly and Dimitar Berbatov. Spurs then gained revenge for the defeat at Upton Park on the final day of the previous season when they beat West Ham at the Lane, and the 5–0 drubbing of the MK Dons in the League Cup extended the unbeaten run to six games. A goalless draw at Vicarage Road against Watford and a 3–1 victory over Belgian side Bruges in early November in the UEFA Cup extended the sequence to eight.

Jol's team were flying but next up were Chelsea. Spurs had not beaten the Blues at White Hart Lane since 1987 and they had failed to take three points from their London rivals since the inception of the Premiership. It was time for a change.

With such high stakes, both sides would have been forgiven for sacrificing quality in search of supremacy, but it was actually a feast of football as the two London teams probed and parried to entertain a capacity White Hart Lane crowd. The visitors almost took the lead after 13 minutes when Arjen Robben burst through, only to be thwarted by Ledley with a trademark last-ditch tackle, but the skipper could do nothing about the Chelsea opener two minutes later when Claude Makelele beat Paul Robinson with a 25-yard volley. The lead was to last a mere ten minutes as Michael Dawson got his head to Jermaine Jenas' free-kick and the two teams went in at the break all square.

The second-half was just as dramatic. Both sides were intent on victory and Tottenham put themselves in the driving seat on 52 minutes with a sublime display of control from Aaron Lennon as the winger brought down Robbie Keane's cross with one deft touch, beat the defence and fired home with the outside of his boot.

Chelsea captain John Terry was sent off late in the game for his second yellow card, but Tottenham still had to endure several scares before the referee finally blew his whistle and they had their long overdue win over their west London rivals.

Although there had been eight bookings in the game – along with Terry's dismissal – it had been a fantastic spectacle and, in the process, Ledley became the first Spurs skipper to lead his team to a league victory over Chelsea in 19 long years. The captain, of course, was already thinking ahead to the next Premiership game. 'It was always going to be difficult... you could see that we were up for it and it was a great all-round performance. For us, it was another game, we take one game at a time and we happened to be playing Chelsea,' he said. 'We wanted the points as much as we will in our next league game.'

Victory over Port Vale in the fourth round of the League Cup took the unbeaten run into double figures but it finally came to an abrupt end at the Madejski Stadium against Reading in mid-November with a 3–1 reverse. But Tottenham under Jol were now made of sterner stuff and they bounced back from their loss at the Royals with an impressive UEFA Cup win over Bayer Leverkusen in Germany, courtesy of a Dimitar Berbatov goal against his former club.

In the league, however, a 3–0 defeat to Arsenal at the Emirates took some of the gloss off the team's recent, run but when Dinamo Bucharest were beaten 3–1 at the Lane in December to confirm Spurs' place in the last 32 of the

UEFA Cup and preserve their unbeaten European record, there was a renewed sense of optimism. The frenetic festive programme was now approaching and, after a rocky start to the season, Tottenham had turned around their Premiership form and convincingly progressed through to the knockout stages of the UEFA Cup.

Ledley played in the defeat at Newcastle two days before Christmas and was in characteristically commanding mood in the Boxing Day victory over Villa at the Lane but, with the New Year approaching, the captain was about to suffer another cruel twist of fate. He had broken his metatarsal the previous season and, as Spurs prepared to face Liverpool, the club revealed he had bruised the foot again and would be unavailable for the match.

'Ledley has very slight bone bruising on his left foot,' Jol explained. 'We are acting sensibly in giving him rest so that he can heal quickly from this minor injury. It is better that we take this precaution rather than having the possibility of a fracture happening and him being out for over two months. This way we can ensure he is back on the pitch and fully fit very soon.'

The foot, however, stubbornly refused to heal and, as the weeks came and went and Ledley still hadn't return to the fray, the club's medical staff decided to send him for a scan in early February that revealed a stress injury to the fourth metatarsal in his left foot – the same bone that denied him a place at the World Cup the previous summer. It was not fractured as before, but Ledley was facing another prolonged and frustrating spell on the sidelines.

It was April before he was finally declared fit to play and Jol decided to gamble on his fitness in a crunch UEFA Cup game. During Ledley's rehabilitation, Spurs had been given a bye in the last 32 of the competition after Dutch side Feyenoord were thrown out following crowd trouble during an earlier game. Tottenham disposed of Braga in the last sixteen and went on to face defending champions Sevilla in the quarter-finals, but lost 2–1 in the first leg in Spain. The second leg at the Lane was looming and Jol, desperate to overturn the deficit, brought his skipper back into the side.

'We've missed Ledley's captaincy but also what he brings as a man and a defender, and having him back will be a big thing for us,' assistant manager Chris Hughton told the *Mirror* before the match. 'Nobody has been more frustrated than Ledley at being out and he is absolutely desperate to show what he can do for us. I can't speak highly enough of the qualities he will give us. The people who have filled in have done a great job but Ledley is our captain and has great respect from everybody and we have missed him.'

Ledley received a standing ovation from the Spurs faithful when he ran out for the game but there was little time for sentimentality once the whistle blew as Sevilla immediately set about the home side in search of an away goal. Ledley was called into action in the second minute when he headed away Dani Alves' dangerous free-kick but the ball did find the back of the net from the resulting corner as Steed Malbranque got an unwitting touch for a disastrous own-goal. Spurs were on the ropes and the visitors doubled their lead five minutes later when former Tottenham striker Freddie Kanouté embarked on a mazy run and beat Paul Robinson from close range.

It was 4–1 on aggregate to Sevilla and Jol's men looked dead and buried. There were no more goals in the first half and, after the break, Spurs showed their character as they poured forward in a bid to save the tie. Jermain Defoe grabbed a goal back just after the hour and, when Aaron Lennon made it 2–2 on the night, the crowd began to sense a dramatic comeback, but Sevilla were not to be denied and the game ended in a draw. Tottenham paid a heavy price for the two early goals and their long-awaited European adventure was over.

'We wanted to come out all guns blazing, but maybe we needed to calm down a little bit,' Ledley said after the game. 'Going behind so early was a bit of a nightmare and, to be honest, we never really recovered. We were all over the place and in shock because we really believed we would come out and start so fast and were looking to do to them what they ended up doing to us.

'I'm nowhere near 100 per cent, but with the team missing so many defenders and with my desire to lift the Cup, I thought I could come in and do well. I've missed playing and I want to help the team as much as I can. Hopefully, I can play again so I can be ready for next season.'

The Premiership was now the club's sole focus. Ledley had lasted the full 90 minutes against Sevilla but sat out the subsequent 3–3 draw with Wigan – a result which left the team in eighth place. There were five Premiership games left and, if Tottenham wanted to play in Europe again, they needed to finish seventh or better. The pressure was on.

The first game of the all-important run-in was the north London derby against Arsenal at the Lane. The Gunners had denied Spurs a place in the League Cup Final earlier in the season and talk of revenge was in the air. The match began at a frenetic pace and then quickened and it was Tottenham who drew first blood on the half-hour with a close-range header. The lead was preserved into the second half but goals from Kolo Touré and Emmanuel Adebayor gave the visitors the edge; as the final whistle loomed, Tottenham appeared dead and buried. There was time for one final attack and, when Jermaine Jenas collected possession 30 yards out, the crowd collectively urged him to shoot. He took their advice and unleashed a powerful, low drive that beat Jens Lehmann and earned his side a precious point.

One point became three after the side's impressive 2–3 win over Middlesbrough at the Riverside, and Spurs recorded back-to-back wins on the road after beating Charlton at the Valley, a result which confirmed the Addicks' relegation from the Premiership. There were just two games left – Blackburn and Manchester City at the Lane – and the team's European destiny was now in their own hands.

The Rovers clash was the 1000th game televised by Sky but, in truth, it was not the spectacle the occasion warranted as both sides struggled to come to terms with conditions at a rain-sodden White Hart Lane. Chances at either end were at a premium but South African striker Benni McCarthy finally enlivened the game on the half-hour when he headed home at the far post and Tottenham's UEFA Cup aspirations were hanging by a thread. Jol's team were not lacking in effort but they were uncharacteristically disjointed going forward and it wasn't until midway through the second half that they were on terms when Jermain Defoe pounced on a loose ball after Dimitar Berbatov's fierce shot was spilled by the goalkeeper. The match ended in a draw and Spurs prepared for the climax of the season knowing a point from their game with Manchester City would be enough to ensure European football in N17 again.

Twelve months earlier, a mystery virus had ravaged the first-team squad and ultimately cost Spurs a top-four finish but, a year later, there were no such dramas as Tottenham came out against City fighting fit and determined to get the job done. Any nerves the team – or the fans – had were quickly dispelled when Robbie Keane celebrated his 200th appearance for the club with a fine volley after just ten minutes. Berbatov made it two 20 minutes later and, although Emile Mpenza pulled one back for the visitors before half-time, Tottenham never looked in danger of being overhauled and could even afford a missed Defoe penalty late on. When the final whistle blew to signal the end of the Premiership season, Spurs were 2–1 winners and back in the UEFA Cup. In fact, Everton's failure to take three points from Chelsea at Stamford Bridge meant that Tottenham finished fifth for a second successive season and could look forward to back-to-back European campaigns for the first time in 20 years.

'The players have certainly earned their rest this summer,' Jol said in his end-of-season report on the club website. 'We have played 59 games this season – more than any Spurs side has played for fifteen years – and the boys have shown real character and resilience at times. I am very proud of them. I've told the players to enjoy their holiday, take a couple of weeks off and then start to get themselves fit for our first training session back.'

Before Ledley could pack his suitcase, however, there was international duty to attend to. England were scheduled to play a high-profile friendly at the rebuilt Wembley against Brazil followed by a Euro 2008 qualifier in Estonia five days later. Ledley's last England appearance had been his Man of the Match performance against Macedonia in October, but Steve McClaren was quick to recall him as he prepared for Brazil and, more importantly, a crucial match in Tallinn.

The Spurs skipper had played in the England B international against Albania at the end of May and the England coach decided to start him against the Brazilians at Wembley alongside John Terry. It was England's first game at their spiritual home in north London after the famous old stadium had been demolished to make way for the new 90,000-capacity ground, but McClaren's charges couldn't quite christen the new arena with a victory.

Brazil were the more fluent side in the early exchanges but it was goalless at half-time as Ledley and Terry repelled the visitors' attacks and gave England a platform from which they could build. The breakthrough finally came in the second period when the Chelsea captain got his head to David Beckham's free-kick and scored the first England goal at the new Wembley. England fans celebrated and, as the final whistle drew closer, it seemed the team would get the victory the script demanded. But it was not to be and when Gilberto Silva crossed into the area in the dying seconds, substitute striker Ribas Diego was first to the ball and headed the equaliser past Paul Robinson.

'We got the performance against a very, very good team, one of the top teams in the world,' McClaren said after the game. 'To nearly get the clean sheet, to be fifteen seconds away, shows that, as a team, we defended well. We saw that attitude, passion, tackles going in and we played good football as well. They came together as a team.'

It was not the win they wanted but, nonetheless, they headed to Estonia in confident mood and the coach opted to retain Ledley and Terry in central defence. It was, in truth, one of the quietest 90 minutes of international football for the Tottenham captain – who won his nineteenth cap in Tallinn – as England dominated from the start and cruised to a 3–0 win courtesy of goals from Joe Cole, Peter Crouch and Michael Owen. England had the three points they needed and the players could finally put their feet up for a few short weeks before the new season was upon them.

For Ledley, it had been another long, injury-affected campaign but, ultimately, another successful one. Under his captaincy, Spurs had maintained their impressive progress in the Premiership with another fifth-place finish and the team were back in Europe. Their run in the UEFA Cup had only been halted by the eventual winners Sevilla and Ledley had forced his way back into the England side with a string of impressive performances that had established him as one of the finest centre-halves in Europe. At the age of 26, his best years were still ahead of him and, with a new, long-term contract with Tottenham signed, sealed and delivered, the future was bright. The King of the Lane was destined for a long and successful reign.

EPILOGUE

Ledley King signed off the 2006/07 season with a typically assured and commanding display against Estonia in Tallinn, but the player and Spurs were to pay a high price for his international exploits. His left knee was once again troubling him and, when he returned to White Hart Lane for treatment, the club medical staff discovered he had aggravated a tear to his cartilage and the only answer was surgery. It was a devastating diagnosis and, while the rest of the Tottenham squad were recharging their batteries in readiness for a new season, Ledley was in hospital under the surgeon's knife. Yet again, the Spurs skipper would spend the summer battling to regain full fitness and take his rightful place at the heart of the Tottenham defence.

The operation went according to plan but the 26-year-old was robbed of his pre-season and, as Spurs began their 2007/08 campaign in August, their inspirational captain was still sidelined. The knee was stubbornly refusing to heal fully and his long-awaited comeback was repeatedly delayed.

Media speculation that the England star had suffered a major setback was rife and, in September, the club was forced to issue a statement denying the rumours, insisting their skipper's rehabilitation was firmly on schedule. Without him in the side, Tottenham made a poor start to their bid to break into the top four of the rebranded Premier League. Ledley's injury deprived the team of their best player but, after having battled back to full fitness more than once in his career, the England star was not daunted by the task ahead of him. The resolve of the Tottenham skipper was legendary, and his skill unquestioned – sooner or later, fans of Tottenham and England would once again relish the return of the King.

APPENDIX

CAREER STATISTICS

Full Name: Ledley Brenton King.
Date of Birth: 12 October 1980, London

First Team Debut: 1 May, 1999 (Liverpool 3 Tottenham 2)
League Appearances: 191 (7 goals)
FA Cup Appearances: 17 (3 goals)
League Cup Appearances: 15 (1 goal)
European Appearances: 6

PREMIER LEAGUE APPEARANCES SEASON-BY-SEASON

1998–99: 1
1999–00: 3
2000–01: 18 (1 goal)
2001–02: 32
2002–03: 25

2003–04: 29 (1 goal)
2004–05: 38 (2 goals)
2005–06: 26 (3 goals)
2006–07: 21

INTERNATIONAL CAREER

England Under-16 caps: 4 (début vs France, 28 September, 1996)

England Under-18 caps: 3 (début vs Spain, 8 March, 1999)

England Under-21 caps: 12 (début vs Luxembourg, 3 September, 1999)

Full England caps: 19 (début vs Italy, 27 March, 2002)